OUT
OF THE
ASHES

C015222336

To my mother and father,
for their strength and courage

Britain after the riots

DAVID LAMMY

guardianbooks

Published by Guardian Books 2011

4 6 8 10 9 7 5 3

First published in Great Britain in 2011 by
Guardian Books
Kings Place, 90 York Way
London N1 9GU

www.guardianbooks.co.uk

A CIP catalogue record for this book
is available from the British Library

ISBN 978-0852-65267-1

Cover image © Matthew Lloyd/Getty Images
Text design by seagulls.net
Cover design by Two Associates

CONTENTS

INTRODUCTION

Last time there were riots in Tottenham I was 13. They took place on the Broadwater Farm estate, just yards away from our family home.

In 1985 it was not uncommon for the police to knock on our front door. My mother spent much of her time worrying that one day it would be officers bearing bad news, rather than asking for information. My eldest cousin and her family lived on Broadwater Farm and I'd end up spending most afternoons there while my parents were still at work. Neighbours and friends would drift in and out of trouble, getting into scraps with the police. Some were caught up in the riots that October and it was a nervous wait before I could be sure that my own brothers were not. Like everyone else, I was shaken to the core by the scale of the violence. Sixty-nine arrests.[1] Hundreds injured.[2] One police officer killed. But the riots were not a bolt from the blue. Inner-city streets had already erupted just a few days earlier, first in Handsworth and then Brixton.

In our neighbourhood tensions had been building for years. My biggest fear growing up was not bigger kids or even National Front bullies, but rather that I would end up in prison. That was the fate of growing numbers of my peers. In many homes, father figures were missing as families crumpled under the stress of economic hardship. In schools, achievement was dragged down by a culture of low expectations, with large numbers streamed off to do CSEs rather than O-levels, or fobbed off with places on the dead-end Youth Training Scheme. Work was scarce. Street life was tough, with the less savvy always at risk of being relieved of their cash or jewellery by youths that everyone knew not to mess with.

The police, meanwhile, often seemed less like protectors and more like an occupying force. Racism was rife and it was common to be stopped, searched and often humiliated. There was a real them-and-us mentality: we withdrew cooperation and they withdrew respect. This is not to say my childhood was unhappy. It wasn't. I got on with the life I had and, like everyone, had good days and bad. But during hot summers, in a deprived area, at a time of recession, confrontation never seemed that far away.

My X-Factor moment came in May 1982. That month I auditioned for a scholarship to become a chorister at Peterborough cathedral and a boarder at the cathedral school King's. My route to success had been plotted by my primary school music teacher and the local vicar. They had decided that I could be a black Aled Jones – the choir boy from Bangor cathedral who had gone to number one in the charts. My mum had grabbed the idea with both hands, determined that I would get the best schooling she could possibly find. This was my opportunity to rise above the canopy that was life back home. I took it but I was half expecting my contemporaries in Tottenham to join me. They didn't, and I was left to navigate this brand new world on my own.

The riots took place in term time, meaning I was away from Tottenham. I watched in horror as the television showed my neighbourhood going up in flames. The murder of PC Keith Blakelock, who suffered more than 40 wounds as he was hacked to death by a mob, left me speechless. Against a backdrop of baton-wielding police and the smouldering embers of burned-out cars, my hometown was engulfed by chaos and violence.

As the de facto ambassador for Tottenham at King's, it fell to me to defend, or at least contextualise, what was going on back home. What I could not articulate at the time was that the Broadwater riots had exposed deep fault lines between the local black youths and their own government. Each time I tried to explain, I stumbled over my words. In many attempts, I never managed to convince a sceptical audience that Tottenham, while often tense, was usually nothing like this.

A quarter of a century later, after another set of riots, I was representing Tottenham for real. Rather than talking to teachers and classmates, I was answering calls from constituents and taking questions from the world's media. This time I was determined to express properly what I could not in 1985: that the overwhelming majority of people in Tottenham rejected the violence, that most had not attacked police officers or looted shops but stayed at home, fearful and upset, that Tottenham is an area of good people, often leading difficult lives – and that they should not be tarnished by the actions of a mindless few.

I remembered well the stigma that had attached itself to Tottenham following the 1980s riots. As the chasm between local and national politicians opened up, no government minister would visit the area, let alone Broadwater Farm, for years. As the television cameras moved on, the community felt forgotten and abandoned. Anyone applying for a job outside the area, a place at university or a mortgage knew the N17 postcode would count against them. It would leap out from an application form. If you did get called for an interview, you would pray the person on the other side of the desk was a football fan. A conversation about Tottenham Hotspur was the best chance of avoiding a series of leading questions about the riots.

All this rushed through my mind as I stood in front of a pack of TV cameras on Tottenham High Road on the morning of 7 August, after the first night of the 2011 riots. A few hundred people had just caused chaos, but there are almost 40,000 people under the age of 25 living in Tottenham.[3] The overwhelming majority were victims, not perpetrators. Above all I was determined to communicate one thing: this was not the true face of our area.

Lighting the touchpaper

The trigger for the violence in 2011 was the death of Mark Duggan. I first caught wind of the incident on the night of 4 August, a Thursday. Immediately, I was worried. I had left three days earlier for a short holiday. Nicola, my wife, and I had been looking forward to a summer without the stresses and strains we had become used to on breaks like this. For the first six years of our married life, I had been a government minister. Piles of briefing papers would follow us wherever we went on holiday. I would be glued to my phone, keeping up with the news. Calls would come in at all hours from civil servants and special advisers, reporting one crisis or another. This year it would be different. Unlike last summer, when I was still coming to terms with Labour's election defeat, we would have some proper family time.

That idea evaporated the moment I took a call from the borough commander in Tottenham. It is not uncommon for a junior officer to ring when there is an incident – a stabbing, a murder or a child protection case. But when you have the most senior officer in the area on the line you know something very serious has happened. Her voice sounded strained and nervous. A man in Tottenham had been shot and killed, she explained, by officers from Operation Trident – the specialist unit that investigates gun crime in the black community across London. The name of the deceased was Mark Duggan. And he was a local resident.

My heart sank. As I put the phone down I turned immediately to Nicola. "I have to get back to Tottenham." At seven the next morning I was boarding a train to London, my mind whirring about the implications of the shooting. By this point news of the incident had gone national. There were reports in the media that three shots had been fired and that a bullet had been found lodged in a policeman's radio.[4] I headed straight for the Ferry Lane estate, where Mark Duggan had died, and then on to

Broadwater Farm, where he had grown up. The area where the shooting had taken place was covered in police tape, much to the annoyance of residents who were having their Friday morning disrupted by a no-go area.

I decided to spend some time talking to the young people who were hovering around the police cordon, to see if I could get a sense of the mood. I knew that an event like this had the potential to light the touchpaper. In 2010 I had been to a memorial service for PC Blakelock, marking the 25th anniversary of his passing. That year there were 10 arrests in connection with his death.[5] Two decades after the Court of Appeal overturned the wrongful murder convictions of the "Tottenham Three", [6] the 1985 riots remained a sensitive issue. The killing of Mark Duggan could put years of progress at risk.

The signs were not good. Both estates were already awash with rumours about what had happened the night before. While the national press was giving the impression of a shootout between the police and a suspect, local youths had a different story. Many had known Mark Duggan. There was talk of him being "executed", with some insisting that he had been unarmed. Local kids who had got off a bus going past the scene of the incident the night before claimed that they had been ushered away by police officers, with some having their cameraphones confiscated. Separating fact from fiction was not going to be easy – and I could see the danger of a gap opening up between the official story and the rumours on the street.

The rumours had me thinking about the Lozells race riots in Birmingham in 2005, which had been sparked by apparently unsubstantiated rumours that a black woman had been raped by a group of Asian men. Black youths had taken to the streets on "revenge" missions, with skirmishes spiralling into full-scale riots. On the Ferry Lane and Broadwater Farm estates no one was talking about rioting, to me at least, but there was a feverish atmosphere that made me nervous.

That morning I put out a statement to the media: "I am shocked and deeply worried by this news. There is now a mood of anxiety in the local community but everyone must remain calm. It is encouraging that the Independent Police Complaints Commission has immediately taken over the investigation. There is a need to clarify the facts and to move quickly to allay fears. It is very important that our community remains calm and allows the investigation to take its course."

I then spent the afternoon making calls. The first was to the IPCC, urging it to publish the ballistics report quickly. It was vital to at least begin establishing some clarity about what had happened on the Thursday night. Next were community figures who I trusted to give me an unedited version of what was going on at street level. Their feedback didn't do much to reassure me. As I had done that morning, they were picking up a lot of anger. All that any of us could do was appeal for calm and wait, hoping that the swirl of rumour and discontent would not spill over into violence.

On Friday night there was calm, but also a sense of deep unease. The intrigue, the anger, the suspicion – call it what you want – was spreading through Tottenham like wildfire. The police's unwillingness to divulge any more details and the IPCC's absence from the TV and radio meant there was little information to counter the speculation.

At around 5.30 on Saturday afternoon, two days after the shooting, a group of about 120 protestors arrived at Tottenham police station, having marched from Broadwater Farm. By this stage people were not just angry and upset at the loss of life. They were incensed at the treatment of the Duggan family. Mark Duggan's girlfriend, the mother of his children, had been informed of his death by the police, but his parents had received no such courtesy. They had learned about the loss of their son via the media. It was a huge mistake on the part of the police. Family and friends had decided to organise a demonstration demanding answers.

Tottenham is no stranger to marches on the police station. These are quasi-scripted exchanges between the community and those that police them. The protestors will stand outside demanding answers, and a high-ranking police official will invite the most immediately aggrieved inside, defusing the anger in the crowd. Except that on this occasion, that didn't occur. The march arrived outside and the family demanded to speak to an officer who could tell them what had happened to their son. The officer put forward, a chief inspector, did not meet the family's expectations of seniority and they were asked to wait. And they waited. According to some accounts, they waited as long as five hours for the promised superintendent to make an appearance.

At 8.30 that evening I received another phone call, this time from a chief inspector, with the news that the police station had come under attack. A squad car parked at the end of the street to divert traffic away from the protest had been hijacked and set alight by a gang of youths. Two officers had fled the scene fearing for their lives.

The group that had marched peacefully was beginning to see the protest taken over by more sinister elements determined to cause trouble. While many will have known Mark Duggan, and no doubt been aggrieved by his death, others were simply there because they saw the police on the back foot. Stones and bottles were thrown at the police station. Around an hour later a second call came through with the news that another police car, and now a bus, had been torched. Tottenham was descending into violence once again. I had been predicting social unrest for a year now, but never had I expected it to come so soon, prove so violent, or begin so close to home.[7]

A tale of two riots

On the surface the riots of 1985 and 2011 were eerily similar. The trigger for both was a police action. In 2011 Mark Duggan had lost his life after being stopped by the police while travelling in a minicab. In 1985 Cynthia Jarrett, a 49-year-old black woman, had suffered a fatal stroke after police burst through her front door to search her home while her son was being held in custody. [8]

But there were important differences. In 1985 it was local officers who entered the home of Cynthia Jarrett. In 2011 the local force didn't know that Operation Trident was on their patch. Had it done, the local police might have told Trident to proceed with greater caution. 1985 was a race riot, given its energy by an explosive relationship between the black community and the police. In 2011 tensions lingered but the relationship between the local force and the local community had improved immeasurably.

Once the trouble started, most people, the black community included, wanted nothing more than to be protected by the police. 1985 involved youths who, almost exclusively, came from Tottenham itself. It was almost a territorial battle. In 2011 the police told me that roughly half of those arrested in the area were not from Tottenham at all – as news of lawlessness spread, criminals from all over London swarmed into the area.

Most fundamentally, those who marched to Tottenham police station that afternoon wanted to lodge a peaceful protest, not to start a riot. Their aim was to pursue justice, not loot shops and burn down buildings. As the Duggan family themselves put it in a television interview, "We do not condone what happened. We are peaceful people... We are grieving and just trying to come to terms with everything that has happened. We do not want this happening in his name."[9] On Monday the BBC was still describing gangs of youths who robbed shopkeepers along Tottenham High Road as 'protestors'.[10] They were nothing of the sort.

I have reviewed the police footage of some of the violence that night. It contains some of the most shocking, most depressing, most shameful behaviour that I have seen. As I sat down to watch the tape, a 12-minute compilation of evidence being used in court, the superintendent warned me some of it would come as a shock. It scarcely prepared me for what I was about to see.

This footage, collected from police cameras and a police helicopter, captured what the Sky and BBC News cameras couldn't. It had been filmed with the intention of collecting proof to arrest and convict the rioters, but it had managed to capture their facial expressions and their voices as they attacked shops and the police. As I watched I expected the faces of rioters to be filled with rage and resentment. If not avenging the death of Mark Duggan, perhaps they were seething at previous treatment by police, or the humiliations of poverty and disadvantage. How else could you explain the ferocity with which they attacked the police, if not anger?

The video depicted a far more sinister emotion: happiness. As the unrest grew and police lines formed, individuals would begin to venture out from the pack to throw a bottle or a brick. They would be goaded on by the gallery behind them, revelling in the entertainment. Youths would laugh as they launched another round of missiles at officers sheltering behind riot shields. In one scene, a heavily outnumbered police line retreats slowly as it is pelted with debris from the street. One rioter has picked up a fire extinguisher and is ready to throw it. He begins to shadow the police cameraman, who visibly flinches as the rioter menaces him with the red barrel. Each time the crowd can be heard to laugh. Eventually a group of rioters charges the police line and the fire extinguisher is thrown. It reaches its target and the policeman is knocked to the ground. The gallery laughs once again.

As the night progresses, the methodical nature of some of the destruction is all too apparent. By a couple of hours into the violence, people have begun turning up in cars to take part in the looting. Outside the council offices, a rioter attempts to set fire to the building. He casually rips up pieces of paper, sets them alight and carefully arranges them as if preparing a barbecue. There is no frenzy. Those around him seem unfazed. They carry on vandalising and stealing from shops along the street.

In the days that followed the rioting, I was among many who described the actions of those involved as mindless. Certainly there were those who were swept along by the crowd, making the biggest mistake of their lives. But plenty of what went on was not spontaneous and unthinking – it was cruel and calculating.

Those who put others' lives and livelihoods at risk were not doing so in the name of justice. The 2011 riots had little, if anything, to do with Operation Trident, the treatment of a grieving family, or a peaceful protest led by women with children in pushchairs.

The events of those few days had tragic echoes of 1985, with the death of a local resident precipitating a night of unthinkable violence. But as Pauline Pearce, a black grandmother living in Hackney, put it on the Monday evening as she scolded youths looting her area, "This is about a fuckin' man who got shot in Tottenham, this ain't about havin' fun on the road and bustin' up the place." One family's grief was hijacked by those determined to wreak havoc and steal from others. That week copycat incidents took place around England. The looters were not restricted to one race, let alone one area. I suspect many of those who took part in Hackney, Enfield, Woolwich and Croydon, let alone Birmingham, Manchester and Nottingham, had never even heard of Mark Duggan.

This book

In the weeks following the riots I barely slept. The atmosphere in Tottenham was incredibly tense. Shops were boarded up. The rubble of the old Carpetright store, the Aldi supermarket and the post office were weeping wounds for the community. The rest of the summer was punctuated with potential flashpoints. The wake for Mark Duggan and then the funeral a month later seemed to have the community on a cliff edge. Even the weekend of the Notting Hill carnival became something to anticipate, as opposed to look forward to. The minute I let myself believe that stability – if not normality – had returned, a walk up the High Road or a fractious public meeting would be a jolt back to reality.

Then was not the time to dig too deeply into the "causes" of what were criminal acts. But, while the events of August 2011 are still fresh in the mind, this remains a conversation we must have, not just in Tottenham but across Britain. Four nights of lawlessness and violence cannot be allowed to simply fade into the memory. Tottenham has now had two riots in a generation. The first was a disaster, the second felt utterly catastrophic, and it is hard to fathom the consequences of a third. Lessons must be learned.

Having that discussion does not mean making excuses for those who revelled in the mayhem. Everyone made their own moral choice – each looter, each rioter, each arsonist has what they did on their own conscience. What my constituents want most of all is that those people be held to account. However, as the prime minister once said, "Understanding the background, the reasons, the causes – it doesn't excuse the crime but it will help us tackle it."[11] This book is my attempt to offer an explanation for the riots. It explores why they happened, what I think they tell us about Britain and where we should go from here.

My argument is that the backdrop to these riots was two revolutions with which Britain has yet to come to terms.[12]

The first was social and cultural: the social liberalism of the 1960s. The second was economic: the free market, liberal revolution of the 1980s. Together they made Britain a wealthier and more tolerant nation. But they have come at a cost, combining to create a hyper-individualistic culture, in which we do not treat each other well.

The riots were an explosion of hedonism and nihilism. People with little to lose lashed out at authority and took what they wanted. The violence and the looting were driven by the sense that, for a few nights only, people could do whatever they pleased. Lives and livelihoods were treated as collateral damage in the pursuit of self-gratification. It is this culture that must be challenged if we are to prevent these scenes from happening again. People need a proper stake in society and a much deeper sense of responsibility towards others.

Two revolutions

In many ways these two revolutions are so embedded in our lives that we barely notice them.

Today most people take for granted that governments should secure people's rights against racism, sexism or any other form of discrimination. But for a large part of my youth this was not the case. The report into the Toxteth riots of 1981 described "horrific" racism as the backdrop to the violence in Liverpool.[13] The Scarman report into the Brixton riots of the same year warned against racial disadvantage becoming an "endemic, ineradicable disease".[14] The Gifford report after Broadwater Farm was deeply critical of a Metropolitan police that employed just 180 ethnic minority police officers at the time.[15]

Even while I was at university progress against these things felt like an uphill struggle. It took six years for the Tottenham Three to be acquitted after their wrongful conviction. As late as 1999 Sir William Macpherson was warning against institutional racism following the treatment of the Lawrence family after their son Stephen was murdered.[16] The battles against discrimination of all kinds are not over, but it is a measure of how Britain has changed that race relations laws, civil partnerships and equal pay acts are now part of our social fabric.

Likewise, a market economy today feels much like the weather – not something anyone has chosen, just part of the background to life in Britain. The big question in politics is how we civilise capitalism, not whether or not to abolish it. But when I turned 17 the Berlin wall was still standing. Then, when Labour politicians described themselves as socialists they really meant it – not in the "values" sense but in the "nationalising industries" sense.

Nor do I take the achievements of these two liberalisms for granted. My mother arrived in Britain in 1970 – the same year as the Equal Pay Act, and just two years on from Enoch Powell's "rivers of blood" speech. When I was 12 my father left for America, leaving her to cope with five children on her own. I soon came to appreciate the liberal voices who wanted to stand up for families like ours. And I don't take lightly the creative genius of a market economy. I served as a minister in the Blair and Brown governments precisely because I believe in the dynamism and opportunities that it can bring.

But these two revolutions, built around notions of personal freedom, sell Britain short unless they are moderated by other forces. The riots were a reminder that, whether we like it or not, we are heavily dependent on one another. We are not born free, as we like to believe, but dependent on our parents. As we grow older, a good life depends in large part on the strength of our relationships with family, friends, neighbours, colleagues and strangers. It is contingent on a society characterised not just by liberty but by mutual respect and mutual responsibility. When this breaks down it takes a lot more than police officers to put things right. My concern is that while we may be less judgmental we are also less compassionate, civil and supportive of one another.

I began writing this book months before the riots took place. Following Labour's election defeat I felt strongly that my own side's response to these two revolutions – social and economic – had exposed its limitations. Faced with the problems of an individualistic culture, we turned to government to make society more fair, safe and virtuous. The result was a blizzard of rules, regulations, targets, measurements, instructions, inspections and initiatives. In government Labour passed more crime legislation in 13 years than had been seen in the whole of the previous century. A new offence was created every day for a decade. At one point the Treasury was specifying and monitoring over 600 performance indicators. A new rule or initiative was almost always the answer to every problem.

On many of the official measures life has got better. But too often it felt as if we were nationalising society rather than reinforcing it. New Labour appeared to become interested only in what the state could deliver on its own. With that, our politics lost a language of care, generosity, neighbourliness, compromise and cooperation. We revered public services but spoke too little of public spirit. We became statist because we appeared uninterested in the other forces for good in society.

Nor did I have faith in the present government to find the right responses. The coalition was not a surprise to me: I could see the uniting theme. The Conservatives believe in free markets; the Liberal Democrats believe in free people. Economic and cultural liberalism have come together, perhaps to reshape British politics for good. But for all the coherence of the government's programme, I didn't believe it could fashion a proper response to Britain's problems. I still believe that it lacks the will or the means to stitch society back together.

The events of August 2011 clarified many of the things I was trying to get at. From the absence of boundaries and role models in children's lives, to the absence of work, dignity and opportunity on many of Britain's estates. From a "my rights" attitude in which people hesitate to think of others, to a consumerist culture driven by materialistic values. From community breakdown and social mistrust, to the pressure on the family in a low-wage economy. From racial polarisation and concerns about immigration to class divisions between those branded "chavs" and the rest.

No single political party, no single government and no single factor was to blame for the riots. They were the result of a lethal cocktail of issues. But the riots spell out a fundamental challenge for British politics: to replace a culture in which people simply take what they want with an ethic of give and take, reciprocity, something for something. Government cannot do this alone but nor can we get there without it. Rather than try to replace society, government should seek to reinforce society in everything that it does. This should be the golden thread running through its attitude to families, communities, workplaces, our justice system, taxation, immigration rules and the welfare state.

That work cannot wait. Places like Tottenham were already hurting before the riots. Many of those in power knew this but were content to look the other way. Under the last government progress was too piecemeal, too half-hearted, too slow. Under a new administration the shadow of the financial crisis obscures all other priorities. Our leaders ask themselves only one thing: how do we pay back what we owe? In our public life there is a palpable lack of hope, ambition and imagination. After the riots we must ask ourselves a deeper and more searching question as a society. Out of the ashes, what kind of country do we want to build?

Some names and descriptors have been changed to protect individuals' privacy.

CHAPTER 1

THE THIN BLUE LINE

Why the police can't do it alone

The BlackBerry used to be the phone for City suits. In August 2011 it provided the infrastructure for a riot. Quietly, it has become the phone of choice in the inner city. A third of all kids in Britain who have smartphones own a BlackBerry.[1] The selling point is that not only is the phone itself cheaper than an iPhone or an Android handset – the toys of the middle classes – but its instant messaging service is free. Young people can chat online without building up huge bills.

In the week of the riots, two other features of BlackBerry Messenger (BBM) were critical. First, BBM messages can be broadcast to huge numbers – one message can go instantly to everyone in a person's address book. Second, unlike posts on Twitter, the messages can be encrypted. The BBM social network is invisible to those outside it. So for three days, would-be rioters were able to plan raids with impunity:

"Everyone in edmonton enfield wood green everywhere in north link up at enfield town station at 4 o clock sharp!"

"Start leaving ur yards n linking up with you niggas... bring your ballys [balaclavas] and your bags trollys, cars vans, hammers the lot!! Keep sending this around to bare man, make sure no snitch boys get dis!!!"

"What ever ends your from put your ballys on link up and cause havic, just rob everything. Police can't stop it."

One of those who received these messages was Adam, a young constituent of mine who goes to a local comprehensive. I have known his family for years – his grandma knew my mother and is a pillar in the local community.

Adam, like many of his peers, is a BBM fanatic. When he switched on his phone on the Sunday morning after the riots in Tottenham, the messages started to flood in. With the police presence heightened in Tottenham, Enfield, which is just four miles up the road, was the next target. In that moment he faced a moral choice – to take up the invitation to join in, or to take another path.

He came through the test with flying colours. After reading the messages with horror he went straight to his parents. Within hours the information had been passed by the family to the local police, via a local councillor. Rather than join in with the looting, he had done what he could to help prevent a second night of criminality and mindless destruction.

Countless others failed that test. On Sunday night, Enfield was terrorised by those who answered the BBM call from all over London. In Enfield retail park Comet, Sports Direct and Curry's were all ransacked. On Enfield High Street, 200 youths roamed from shop to shop helping themselves to what they could. Tesco and Starbucks were looted. HMV and T-Mobile stores were vandalised. Fearing the worst, shopkeepers left their businesses early and locked down the shutters, but even this wasn't enough to stop the jewellers being cleaned out as the mob ran amok. Some were gang members – around one in five of those arrested in London has links to gangs[2] – but others were just people who couldn't help themselves. Another community was left shaken to its core by the sense of chaos and lawlessness.

The police were outmanoeuvred mercilessly. For all the advances in community policing, the riots demonstrated real failures in intelligence gathering. Too few people like Adam were willing to come forward. BlackBerry should also have done the responsible thing and suspended its network for those few nights. The inconvenience of a few law-abiding people being unable to send instant messages is incomparable to the damage done that week to property and the social fabric. But more than anything it is the sentiment in the messages that haunts me. "Just rob everything.

Police can't stop it." They reveal something deeply worrying about British society: the only thing preventing a sizeable minority from breaking the law is the fear of being caught.

A huge police response eventually restored order to London's streets after three nights of nihilism. The Metropolitan police briefed the newspapers that rubber bullets could be used for the first time on the British mainland "if deemed necessary".[3] All police leave across the capital was cancelled and extra officers were bussed in from other parts of Britain. Some 16,000 officers took to the streets of London on the Tuesday night – nearly three times as many as the night before.[4]

By neat symmetry, 16,000 is also the total number of police officers projected to leave the forces across England and Wales under planned budget cuts from 2011 to 2014.[5] For the foreseeable future, political debate will focus on numbers – and for good reason. The past decade and a half have demonstrated that hiring more police officers can help cut crime. But the riots were a reminder of something basic about our security: we are policed by consent. There are 375 people for every police officer in Britain.[6] When disorder breaks out, policing must be swift, firm and decisive – far more so than it was those nights. But a civilised and a safe society must be policed not just by uniformed officers, but also by notions of pride, shame, self-restraint and responsibility to others.

Stabbings and tax credits

"Is there anything else you want to talk about, David?" Gordon Brown asked as he wandered over towards me. I had been called in for a breakfast meeting in Downing Street in 2008. It was about nothing in particular. Following Tony Blair's resignation and Gordon's appointment as prime minister, Number 10 had taken to inviting six or seven ministers in at a time for coffee, croissants and a chat. Gordon would make a short opening contribution, setting out what his priorities were, before inviting others to pitch in with any thoughts, suggestions or concerns. It was a worthwhile idea, despite the feeling that you were attending something in between a thinktank seminar, a political strategy meeting and a job interview.

The meeting passed unremarkably. It was at the end of the session that Gordon came over to ask if there was anything in particular that I would like to raise. "Actually, there is," I said, noticing him look alarmed that I might be about to launch into a long speech. "I'm really worried about knife crime." It was still a big concern in Tottenham and was showing all the signs of morphing from an inner city problem to a nationwide concern. More and more mothers were turning up at my weekly advice surgeries and telling me that they felt scared and helpless to stop their sons drifting into trouble.

"What are we doing for these women?" I asked. "Often the father isn't around, and their own parents might be on the other side of the world. They're not coping and we've got to find a way of helping them." Gordon looked at me quizzically while I spoke, as if I was missing something obvious. "Tax credits," he responded, as soon as I finished. "If they're single parents and they're working, they'll be entitled to them." With that there was a pat on the arm. "Thanks, David." On to the next conversation.

I left the meeting downcast. I know as well as anyone what effect material poverty can have on children. Cramped housing gives children nowhere to learn or to play. Poverty starves homes of books and PCs. Scarce resources exclude children from sports clubs, drama classes and scout troops that build character, teach discipline and nurture healthy peer groups. Low pay blackmails parents into accepting another shift at work rather than going home to help with the homework. The lack of any real stake in society – the seemingly remote chance of a decent job or a decent home – creates a dangerous dynamic. Young men and women grow up feeling they have little to lose from chancing their arm at criminality. It is no coincidence that crime is highest in the poorest neighbourhoods.[7] Following the riots the young people who appeared in court were more than twice as likely to be on free school meals than the rest of the school population.[8] But the mothers sitting nervously in front of me in my surgeries were not just talking about money. They were talking about the culture their children grow up in.

What the perfunctory "tax credits" response ignored was that these parents have it far tougher than in the past. Today one in four children is brought up by a single parent, compared with just one in 14 in 1972, the year I was born.[9] Overwhelmingly, it is the father who is absent in those families. Many single mothers do a heroic job looking after their children, as mine did with us; but as she found, it becomes twice as hard to set boundaries with half the number of parents.

Previous generations got by with the help of extended family. Now families are scattered around the country, if not the world, with half of all grandparents living 10 miles or more away from their grandchildren.[10] Not only is the nuclear family withering away; so are the support networks.

Beyond the family home there are no longer the social structures that were once sources of civility. In public spaces, there are fewer figures of authority, from bus conductors to park wardens, to reinforce expectations of decent behaviour. With fewer of us living and working in the same area, we are less likely to recognise our neighbours' children, let alone feel we have the right to tell them off if we see them misbehaving. And as strangers, we shrink from intervening: seven in 10 of us say we would walk on by if we saw a group of children vandalising a bus stop.[11] This is, in part, because of the fear of retaliation, with names like Phillip Lawrence, the headteacher who was stabbed dead after intervening to protect a boy from a gang of youths, etched into our consciousness. But it is also down to the hesitancy that adults now have about interacting with children outside their immediate family, in case their motives are questioned.

Instead, children are socialised by other influences. In Britain they now spend twice as much time in front of a TV or computer screen as they do in the classroom.[12] Many operate for large parts of the day in a peer-to-peer culture online, where adults are almost entirely absent. During the riots, there were few older voices to be heard on the BBM networks. Meanwhile, the consumer pressures on children mount daily, as they are schooled by marketing consultants to believe their worth is determined by what they wear – that they "need" the new trainers or the platinum chain to keep up.

Fuelling this culture of hyper-consumerism is an increasing inability to delay gratification. In a world where everything is available on demand, the idea of working for something, waiting for something and truly earning something is losing currency. Violence is glamorised on TV, on games consoles and in music, where the intricacies of human pursuit are boiled down to "Get rich or die trying." Notions of hard work and graft are undermined by reality TV plucking people from obscurity, propelling them to fame and success overnight. Traditional measures of success are devalued as being unreachable or a betrayal of your true identity. The only honourable and sensible means to riches and success is the fraternity of gangs.

These things are manageable in an affluent household. The goods that you are told that you need and deserve are not out of reach, while consumer influences are moderated by out-of-school classes and activities that teach the virtues of self-discipline and perseverance. But in poverty, when you are told simultaneously that you are worth it and that you can't have it, the inability to delay gratification becomes poisonous. Hustling, running drugs and petty criminality become all the more appealing as shortcuts to power and status. Popular culture provides fun and escapism for the middle classes, but in the inner city it can feel like a call to arms.

This is the cultural cocktail that mothers were worried about. It is what fuelled the riots. But as a society we have yet to find a sufficient response to it. Gordon Brown understood which parents needed help – and recognised the pernicious effect that poverty can have on family life. But his answer betrayed a tendency to see the world through a spreadsheet.

Some of the responses to the looting reveal the same tendency today. There was a class element to the riots, no doubt about it. But those who believe that the disturbances were only about poverty must ask themselves this: why did the majority of youths from deprived areas choose to remain at home and obey the law? Adam's response to the BBM call-outs was not to don a balaclava and head to JD Sports, but to go to his parents. What shields kids in the inner city from this kind of temptation is not just their material circumstances, but strong, healthy relationships with others – with parents, peers, teachers and neighbours.

As these relationships have frayed, government has stepped into the void with more laws, police and powers. CCTV cameras have replaced the watchful eyes of local people. The community support officers are a way of replacing the shopkeeper or school teacher who might once have stepped in to chide a group of misbehaving teenagers. The asbo is used to compensate for a decline in neighbourliness and civility.

The extra police officers have helped. Residents almost

always welcome the security cameras. These things shouldn't be scoffed at. But we have ended up nationalising society rather than bolstering it. The blind faith in tax credits and the obsession with passing more laws come from the same worldview.

It is one that lacks any sense of the individual in context – surrounded by a culture, by relationships with other people, by social norms and expectations of behaviour. The belief is that a mighty central state can manage people's behaviour – the only dispute is whether to use the stick or the carrot.

Some want to deliver order via water cannons and police bullets. Others hope to turn people's lives around by topping up their bank accounts. Neither recognises that people are, at heart, social animals who respond to more than just incentives and penalties. Neither addresses the central problem: a society where too many teenagers grow up without clear boundaries, self-discipline and a sense of right and wrong.

Smacking and Supernanny

Everything starts with the family home. It is where a child's character is formed and boundaries are first established. But in recent years parliament has dedicated more time to telling parents what not to do than to offering practical support.

Most emblematic of this were attempts by MPs to criminalise parents for smacking their children. The proposals, driven by a liberal concern for the rights of the child, were put forward with good intentions. The aim was to protect children from domestic abuse, following a series of high-profile cases in which they suffered terrible cruelty at the hands of their own relatives.

One of those cases was that of Victoria Climbié, who died in my constituency. I insisted on giving evidence in the inquiry into her death. I was horrified that neither doctors nor social services had acted to save a girl who had suffered 128 injuries before she died, aged just eight, of hypothermia and malnutrition. The pathologist who examined her body following her death described it as the worst case of abuse he had ever seen, reporting scars all over her body, from cigarette burns to "weapon-type injuries".

Quite rightly, her suffering created a sense of urgency to do more to protect children from such appalling abuse. Unfortunately, some of that energy was misdirected. The 2004 legislation[13] that followed the Climbié enquiry altered a law that had stood in England since 1860. Until that point, parents had been permitted to use "reasonable chastisement". The legislation changed that to make criminal anything that left more than "temporary reddening of the skin".[14]

This small change in the law fundamentally altered its nature. Previously the law had been based on common sense, placing trust in judges and juries to distinguish between "reasonable chastisement" and abuse. With the new legislation, common sense was replaced by a rule specified from Whitehall that has left parents all over the country terrified that a smack on the bottom of a toddler will land them in court and lose them their children.

Of course society has a duty to prevent the kind of brutality inflicted on Victoria Climbié. But the reason she suffered was not that a jury had been incapable of distinguishing between abuse and discipline. It was that despite warnings from relatives, allegations of child abuse, seven visits from social services and two admissions to hospital, no one took action.

In places like Tottenham, which have been through a series of high-profile child protection cases, this change to the law has had a deeply damaging effect. I remember my own mother panicking after what turned out to be a routine visit from social services shortly after my father left. Worried that "social services" could mean only one thing, she sought a reassurance from her MP that she wouldn't lose her children. Such fears have only grown since 2004. Most parents do not want to smack their children. Many view it as a last resort and even a sign of failure. But following the new law, many of these same people believe that their authority has been shot and they are no longer sovereign in their own homes.

This is a widespread concern, but one felt even more keenly in areas with higher crime rates and lower incomes. The perception of many, reiterated to me after the riots, was that better-off parents can supplement liberal parenting with the disciplined environments of cadet groups, outdoor pursuits, tennis clubs, piano lessons and traditional private schooling. But if you are on the 15th floor of a tower block with drugs and gangs outside you need to be able to set limits. This viewpoint has to be understood by those who live their lives far away from that world. Government must learn to trust the judgment of ordinary people again. The unhelpful and unworkable rules for parents brought in in 2004 should be repealed, returning the law to how it stood for nearly a century and half.

While government officials were busy telling parents what not to do, growing numbers were glued to TV screens watching shows like Supernanny in the hope of some constructive advice. Others were logging onto sites like Mumsnet to pick up tips from one another. Culturally, politics has been miles away from most people's daily concerns.

Now is also the time to rethink what social services really stand for. At present they are an emergency service for the poor and vulnerable. Britain has been left with ghettoised family services, which offer help only in times of crisis, associated in the public mind with Victoria Climbié and, more recently, Baby P.

The long-term goal must be to recast social services as family services: positive, universal and valued. In healthcare we each have a GP who acts as a gatekeeper to other specialists. The same ought to be true for family services. Each family should be able to register at a SureStart centre with a qualified professional, removing at a stroke some of the stigma and fear surrounding asking for help. From the moment a prospective mother and father went in for their first scan, they would know where to go for information, advice and support when they needed it. Parents could be directed towards relationship counselling and peer support. Where relationships break down, separating couples could be helped to sort out how best to care for their children.

Becoming a parent is one of the most significant experiences in life, but it is also the one we feel least prepared for. No one teaches us how to be a good parent. We pick up clues from our own parents and friends, or we read snippets of advice in newspapers, books and magazines. But fundamentally parenting is scary because there is no manual.

It isn't surprising that half of all parents, across all social backgrounds, express an interest in attending parenting classes.[15] A revamped social service would be the means for them to be provided. Opportunities should be made available for parents to learn more about child psychology, nutrition and development. Further education colleges already provide courses on these topics for those who seek a professional qualification, but they are not open to enough of the people who matter most to children: parents.

Of course, it is parents who are responsible for bringing up children, not the government. These courses should not be compulsory.

A holistic family service would be the first step in jettisoning the assumption that family policy is all about toddlers and not adolescents. Parental leave after birth should be matched by the option of a week's leave, shared between parents, as children make the transition between primary and secondary schools. This is the time at which children find themselves faced with new academic demands, strange buildings, new rules, much older peers and the prospect of making an entirely new friendship group. Society must help parents to provide support to their children beyond the early years.

As with smacking, government should intervene in family life when parents are plainly not living up to their responsibilities – for example when children are repeatedly arrested or excluded from school. In these cases, receipt of child benefit should become conditional on parents accepting intensive packages of support to help them restore calm and order in family life. The original intention of the anti-social behaviour order was that sanctions would be coupled with proper support for offenders and their families if necessary. In practice, just 5% of asbos contain measures designed to address the causes of anti-social behaviour.[16] Predictably, more rules could not do the job alone and around half of all asbos have been breached. Getting back to this idea that sanctions and support should come together would restore a much clearer sense of give and take in our welfare state.

In doing so, government must recognise that turning whole families round is not easy. It will not be achieved simply through the threat of sanctions, nor through a trail of children's services queueing up for occasional meetings with "problem families". Progress requires one individual – a qualified professional – to get a grip on the situation and take responsibility. It requires proper coordination of all the support that the family receives and perseverance with the family itself that verges on intrusiveness. When all these things come together, then you have a chance.

Boxing clever

Families cannot do it alone, though. The messages that come from within the home must be reinforced at school if they are to truly shape a child's character. Parents know this. This is the real reason for the scramble for school places. It is the unspoken truth behind the willingness of the middle classes to stretch family finances to pay for private education. Parents are not paying for better teachers, or even necessarily for better facilities. They are paying for an academically competitive peer group and a traditional ethos – one that will reinforce the character traits they have tried to encourage in their children. Many instinctively understand the desire to fit in and be accepted by a group – and the damage that it can do when it pulls children in the wrong direction. Having friends involved in problem behaviour makes young people 50% more likely to be arrested themselves.[17] Disobedience and criminality can spread like a virus.

Just as parents must be sovereign at home, teachers, not children, must run schools. This must include the freedom to remove pupils when they intimidate others and threaten all the work that teachers and head teachers put in. Governments have to stand with the majority of parents – and the majority of children – who want schools to be places of learning, not chaos.

What this cannot mean, however, is simply writing off problem children as lost causes. At the moment, permanent exclusion from school is catastrophic for a child. Nearly a third of offenders were regular truants from school and almost half were excluded.[18] Only one in 15 of those excluded manages five GCSE passes.[19] Three in 10 don't even bother turning up to the pupil referral units run by local authorities.[20] The problem is not that disruptive, troubled kids are removed from schools; it is that there is no decent alternative.

In the shadow of the White Hart Lane stadium, not far from where the looting began in Tottenham, there lies a glimpse of a different way forward. Opposite the stadium stands an unspectacular, shed-like building, home of the London Boxing Academy (LBA). Walk through the entrance and you see teenagers sparring in the middle of a boxing ring, under the eye of a professional coach. Continue into the next room and there is a small group of boys sitting around a table, chatting while they paint. Head upstairs to the ICT suit, or the adjacent classroom, and there is an atmosphere of serenity. The LBA has a zen-like feel to it that defies all your expectations – and probably those of the troubled boys who end up there.

The LBA started as a community project at the turn of the millennium. The idea was that local kids could wander in off the streets and work with the coaches at the amateur boxing club. The boys would join a club rather than a gang, they'd learn to box rather than deal drugs, and they'd be kept busy rather than left to wander the streets. By 2006 the project had bigger ambitions. A donation from Sir Alan Sugar had helped cover the rent for more facilities, while funding from a Westminster thinktank, Civitas, would be used to employ an English and maths teacher on site.

A year later the LBA was registered as a formal charity and had begun taking children from local schools who were on the verge of expulsion. The boys would have a chance to start again without a blot on their records, while the schools would be able to restore some order in their classrooms. What began as an attempt to keep troubled young men off the street for a few hours had become a concerted effort to turn their lives around.

The LBA offers a tough kind of love. If kids don't turn up in the morning, they can count on someone knocking on their front door. A boxer is present in every class, part mentor for the kids and part bodyguard for the teacher. If pupils at the academy want a new pair of boxing gloves to spar with, they must be earned with good attendance and good behaviour. The purpose of the boxing itself is not simply to expend some energy; it is to teach discipline, perseverance and the habit of working at something day after day.

The structure and discipline sit alongside relationships that are warm and caring. Tea and toast are served on the house in the morning and there is genuine respect between the pupils and staff. The aim is that no one leaves the academy without a basic qualification in maths, English and computer literacy. One third of the boys' time is spent boxing, while lessons and tutorials make up the rest. The LBA invests in people's souls as well as their skills. The boys are also there to learn about sexual health, first aid and drug awareness. What is really happening in this small corner of north London is a process of socialisation.

The trick for those who make policy is to ensure that sufficient funding goes into schemes like the London Boxing Academy. The danger is that no one organisation has the incentive to put the money in. The temptation for schools is simply to dump difficult children on the next school rather than fund costly places at institutions like the LBA. Local authorities, meanwhile, actually end up saving money if youths end up in the prison system, which they do not pay for.

We need many, many more places like the LBA. If we are to make sure that resources are provided, we must solve these financial riddles so that schools and local authorities keep some of the money they save from investments that keep people out of the criminal justice system.

Peer pressure

Most days a local policeman drops into the LBA to check on the boys. He sees it as part of his job to help rebuild their relationship with figures of authority, but he also wants to learn more about what is happening on the streets he walks each day. He talks to the boys about their friends, brothers and sisters. He asks what worries them and how the police can help.

The big development of the past decade has been community policing of this sort. It is based on the idea that norms of decent behaviour are best enforced from within a community, that trust is the basis for true authority, that social boundaries are best enforced by people you know. I remember from my own youth the feeling that the police were an occupying force, imposed by those who neither understood nor cared much for our area. That schism fuelled the riots of 1985 and has taken years to close.

The events of August 2011 proved how fragile that progress is. The sense that "the police are the public and the public are the police", as Sir Robert Peel put it, dissipated very quickly. The most frustrating element of this is that it was not local officers who fired the bullet that killed Mark Duggan or who directed the policing of the riots, during which residents felt so abandoned. Mark Duggan was killed by Operation Trident – a specialist cross-London team that focuses on gun crime in black communities – and it was a distant control station that called the shots during the riots.

The response cannot be to give up on community policing. It must be to entrench it much further. In future, local police teams should own their own patches. Police officers who enter neighbourhoods with guns must be alive to local sensitivities. Neither was the case on the evening that left Mark Duggan dead and triggered a disastrous chain of events.

Meanwhile, local forces in inner city areas have to get much more serious about recruiting from the communities that they serve. It takes hardwired knowledge of an area to understand the difference between the gang member causing trouble and the good kid minding his own business on his way home from school.

When officers persistently get these things wrong, stopping innocent people several times in quick succession, they alienate people who should be allies. It fuels the perception held by many black young men that they are damned if they do, damned if they don't. Many are worried about knife crime but resent the inability to distinguish between them and knife-carrying gang members. Officers with better knowledge of their areas would help address this, as would smarter tactics from local teams. A good beat team knows how important it is to foster dialogue with the community, particularly with the young men who are staying out of trouble.

It would also help if the police looked a lot more like the people they have to stop and search. We have come a long way since the 1985 riots, when there were fewer than 200 ethnic minority police officers across the whole of London[21] – but, on pragmatic policing grounds, we have not come far enough. Today it is still the case that one in 10 police officers in London comes from an ethnic minority background, when the figure for the city's wider population is one in four.[22] In places like Tottenham, which contains the most ethnically diverse postcode in the country,[23] this becomes more of an issue still.

Law and order

You need only to look at a map of where the riots took place to recognise that there was a class element to what happened. The unemployment rate in Tottenham is among the highest in the country.[24] In Hackney, where riots broke out the following night, more than one in three children grows up in poverty.[25] These were not riots led by the wealthy. The absence of real opportunities, of meaningful work and of a proper stake in society is an issue that must be addressed. But this alone does not serve as a proper explanation. It does not explain why Adam, my teenage constituent, took one path while countless others took another. There was more to the scenes of destruction than economics.

The police response was leaden-footed and hesitant in parts. People felt abandoned rather than protected in their shops, their homes and their neighbourhoods. But we call it the "thin blue line" for a reason. There must be other forces for law and order in Britain beyond those who are paid to patrol the streets. The riots revealed a take-what-you-can mentality and a horrific indifference towards others. What is needed, more than anything in a more fractured, anonymous and individualistic society, is a sense of responsibility to one another. This must be nurtured in families, cultivated in schools and enforced from within communities themselves.

CHAPTER 2

SHAMELESS

The spectre of the ‘underclass’

I was rushing to meet the Duggans' lawyer. I had not slept. Now Jesse Jackson was on the phone. Amid the sympathy and solidarity the great man expressed was a lament that has rung from his speeches in the decades since he stood alongside Martin Luther King in the battle for equality. The freedoms won for minorities, from discrimination in the workplace, in housing, in the street, on buses, had ushered in a new, more suffocating barrier. Legal racism has fallen away to reveal a world where you are free to be paid less than you need to feed your kids, free to sink as well as to swim, free to rob and loot from one another. It's a speech I've heard Jesse give before – and an effective one.

Almost as soon as he said goodbye, another call came in. I picked it up half expecting Jesse to have a postscript for me, but rather than his South Carolina drawl it was a voice from much closer to home. The prime minister was businesslike. He began by expressing his sorrow at what had happened in Tottenham before moving on to give me reassurances about policing and public order in the days ahead. As we spoke, I recognised in his voice the same heavy burden of responsibility carried by his two Labour predecessors. In times like this people look to prime ministers for action but also for explanation.

The action part he had addressed already. Clearly alive to criticism that he had been slow to take a lead after the rioting began, he had delivered a no-nonsense message from Downing Street that morning, promising that looters and arsonists would be brought to justice. The explanation part could wait a few days, but it would still be expected of him. I already had a pretty good sense of what it would be. “I suspect we’re going to be hearing a lot more about the broken society in the next few days,” I said. “I suspect you may be right,” he replied.

Within days the prime minister had returned to his pre-election narrative with gusto. The broken society was back, serving as a means for the Conservative party to get at Britain’s social problems. In August 2011, however, the story contained a new and striking feature: class. “Parts of our society are frankly sick,” Cameron declared.[1]

In the coming days and weeks, senior figures in government began to flesh out the story. Ken Clarke, normally scornful of hyperbole, used his first public intervention after the riots to lash out at a "feral underclass".[2] Boris Johnson, never too far behind a bandwagon, decided to go one better, lamenting a "feral criminal underclass".[3] Another cabinet minister, Iain Duncan Smith, who had done much of the "broken society" thinking for the Conservatives in opposition, set out his own stall describing "the steady rise of an underclass".[4] This was the day, he argued, when "the inner city came to call" on the rest of society.[5]

Until this point social class had always been implicit in the "broken society" story, gestured at but never tackled directly. References from Conservative front-benchers to "Shameless Britain" and the "Jeremy Kyle generation" pointed, not so subtly, to a particular stratum of society. But the riots were the moment the broken society stopped applying to all of us. Now our political leaders felt they had full permission to let rip into "feral" families. As they did, their reaction to the riots held up a mirror to politics in modern Britain: the party most comfortable talking the language of class is not that of Nye Bevan and Dennis Skinner, but the Tories.

Them and us

The rioters were not exclusively from poor backgrounds. Nor did the vast majority of people from inner city areas get caught up in the violence. It was not that simple – not even close. In any case, statistics do not riot; people do. But the riots did reveal a minority of people, drawn largely from some of the most deprived areas of the country, who did not have a stake in society.

For some the nihilism of the violence was hard to comprehend. Rioters burned down public buildings, from post offices to job centres, that were there to serve them. Some vandalised high streets in their own neighbourhoods. People put out of business shops that they had been relying on for years. As Cameron put it in his statement promising a "fightback", "You are not only wrecking the lives of others, you're not only wrecking your own communities – you are potentially wrecking your own life too."[6] The problem is that the looters did not see it like that. Few felt as if they were part of what they were lashing out at.

The language of a "feral underclass" suggests the feeling is mutual. It sets up a society of "them" and "us" in a way that the "broken society" idea does not. If the whole of society is broken, then we are all implicated in Britain's problems. If the problem can be scaled back to a particular class, things are much easier. The riots were *their* problem, not ours. The grave danger is that the language of the "underclass" perpetuates the problem that it refers to, ghettoising a group of people by ignoring the relationship between them and the rest.

The tragedy of modern Britain is that we have the perfect recipe for what our leaders term the underclass: a working class with no stake in capitalism and a middle class that feels cheated by the welfare state. The working class believe they put into the economy but get little in return. The middle class feel the same about our devalued systems of national insurance. It is this lethal combination that has produced entrenched poverty, the resentment at "chavs" and the shocking, dysfunctional behaviour on display during the riots.

Popular capitalism

It was not supposed to be this way. I remember my mother, who would have proudly described herself as a socialist, sending off for the share brochure when British Gas was privatised in 1986. Like others, she had seen the "Tell Sid" campaign and liked the idea of becoming part-owner of a company for the first time in her life. While Labour was making abstract arguments about the value of nationalisation, people like my mum were at home flicking through the brochures they had received in the post. "Popular capitalism is nothing less than a crusade," Margaret Thatcher declared that year, "to enfranchise the many in the economic life of the nation."[7]

The Thatcherite promise was that we would each have our own stake in the nation's wealth – something to be proud of, something to protect, something to lose. The reality has proven far different. Though the brochure took pride of place on the coffee table in our front room, Mum never got beyond leafing through the pages. Owning shares was a nice idea in theory, but not a practical alternative to paying the bills. The sale of council houses repeated the same story. Electorally the policy was a roaring success, encapsulating a political message of thrift and self-reliance. In the main, those who bought their homes never looked back. But, as with the British Gas shares, buying your council house meant having some money to spend in the first place.

Those who missed the boat as Mrs Thatcher's capitalist ship set sail found themselves in choppy waters. The decline of union power and the disappearance of employment protections from the statute book weakened the hand of employees. The theory was that it would become easier to hire people as well as fire them. The reality was that ordinary employees also lost the power to drive a decent bargain, and wages slipped back for those who relied on them the most. Over the past 30 years, the national share of income going to the bottom half of earners in Britain has fallen by a quarter.[8]

The trends that started during the economic revolution of the 1980s have been given turbo boosters by globalisation. While those at the bottom scrap for jobs on poverty pay, a highly mobile group at the top – traders, lawyers, consultants and accountants – offer their services in a global marketplace rich with opportunity. The difference between a global and a parochial marketplace explains why Tesco's CEO takes home 500 times the pay of someone stacking his shelves.[9] Many have no real assets to speak of. Today more than one in five Britons has no savings at all, while one in three has less than £500 stored away.[10]

In the absence of savings or decent wages, many turn to debt. The same story repeats itself in my weekly advice surgeries, with constituents telling me of loans taken out to pay off loans. The doorstep lenders come round for a cup of tea and hand over a tenner. They offer you a route out. Then the punitive interest rates kick in and another loan is required, from another lender, to cover the costs of the first. Except the second, third and fourth do not bother with the charm offensive. They already have you where they want you. There is no pretence of financial advice, no small talk over tea and biscuits. And people sink and they sink.

All this means that many of the things that used to seem within reach for working-class families – a steady job, some savings and a chance to own your home – have slipped out of reach. The average low- to middle-income household can now expect to wait more than 30 years to build up the deposit needed for a first home.[11] The promise "to enfranchise the many in the economic life of the nation" seems more like a cruel joke. Markets have been freed but those at the bottom don't feel liberated. They are, in Jesse Jackson's phrase, free only to be poor. The riots demonstrated that it is a freedom that many do not prize. Thousands across the country were willing to take their chances during a lawless few days. A criminal record, a spell in prison, the sheer indignity of the looting – none of this was enough to persuade them to respect some of the most basic rules of civilised society.

The bulwark against these temptations has always been working-class respectability. While the upper classes inherited titles and the middle class inherited assets, the working class passed on a different sort of wealth: traditions, values and cultural capital. As my mum used to put it to us, "We may be poor but you can still have pride." In Tottenham this ethic was held together in large part by churches, pastors and youth workers. In other parts of the country the job was done by friendly societies, working men's clubs and trade unions, which reinforced a sense of belonging to something bigger.

Today these wider sources of working-class identity are on the wane. They have been replaced by an impatient consumer ethic that invites us to break free from inherited identities rather than embrace them.

For those who succeed, all of this can be hugely liberating. Horizons expand and people pursue lives and lifestyles that their parents would not have dared aim for. Those who make it are certainly not nostalgic for the days when growing up meant following a path that had already been trodden by your parents and their parents. But there has been a downside too. It is hard to imagine the looting and pillaging of shops in some of Britain's old industrial towns, but life in the modern metropolis offers escape and anonymity. All this heaps pressure on the family as the medium through which values and character are transmitted from one generation to the next. Today, a good family must insulate children from drifting into gang life, or taking easy shortcuts to wealth and status when other routes seem closed off.

For many, the story of one family during the riots summed it up. A teenage girl had been arrested and charged with stealing clothes, make-up and CDs on the first night of disturbances in Tottenham. She turned up to court alone with no parents to escort her. The judge refused to bail her until they arrived, proclaiming that her parents "don't seem to care".[12] The story was picked up by several national newspapers as the perfect example of a dysfunctional teen at the centre of a broken family, headed by incapable parents.

But real life is rarely as simple as the headlines. The family in question were constituents of mine. My office has had contact with them before and has always found them polite and courteous. Their neighbours describe them as decent, church-going people. Both parents work – and hard. One is self-employed, running a small business, while the other is a minicab driver – a job with irregular hours that can stretch late into the night.

Aside from being let down by a local authority that left their child without a school for over a year, they have also had to battle hard to keep their family afloat, working weekends and long hours. It is easy to criticise, but they were not at the pub or lying on the sofa. They were at work, doing their best to make ends meet. They are not the caricatures of the "broken society" or a "sick" underclass but a decent family struggling to cope.

Too often this gets lost. Families do not exist in a vacuum. They are part of a wider economy that makes it either easier or harder to be together. We have an established rhetoric in Britain about "burdens on business" but far too little is said about the burdens on the family that come with low pay and long hours. The Confederation of British Industry (CBI), the biggest lobbying organisation for business in the UK, opposed the introduction of paternity leave in 1997,[13] the introduction of the minimum wage in 1998 and plans to increase the level of it since,[14] the extension of maternity leave in 2005,[15] new flexible working rights for parents in 2008[16] and plans for a shared system of parental leave in 2010.[17] But across Britain today millions of parents find themselves with the cruel choice between making enough money to provide for their children or having enough time to spend with them.

Our political leaders cannot have it both ways – frequently the social conservatism that emphasises the role of the family clashes with economic liberalism that makes family life more difficult. David Cameron, who also opposed the minimum wage on its introduction, has since spoken of a "moral" capitalism, promising to "place the market in a moral framework – even if that means standing up to companies who make life harder for businesses and families."[18] Yet very little has been done to renegotiate the relationship between the family and the workplace. Britain still has among the longest working hours in Europe, while five million employees work on wages that are not sufficient to provide a "minimum acceptable quality of life".[19]

Parents, of course, have their own responsibilities to fulfil. There is an important conversation to be had about parenting that extends beyond time pressures and financial circumstances. But those who run the country have a duty to recognise that while markets have creative genius they can also be destructive of many of the things we value – from the environment to family life.

To lambast "feral" families without having much more to say about untamed capitalism reeks of hypocrisy.

Need versus contribution

For all this, the public reaction to the riots was telling. Most people's immediate concern was not the absence of a popular capitalism, but rather the implications for the welfare state. Polling found a clear majority in favour of stopping welfare benefits for those involved in the disturbances. Nearly half were willing to evict rioters and their families from council homes.[20]

"Benefit in return for contributions, rather than free allowances from the state," declared William Beveridge, the architect of the welfare state. "That is what the people of Britain desire."[21] But the 2011 riots revealed the extent to which people feel that this social contract has broken down.

Just as the vision for a popular capitalism has faded, so too the welfare state has drifted away from its founding principles. A system of national insurance, based on principles of give and take, has gradually been reduced to grudging acts of charity towards the least well off.[22]

The right to buy, the policy most emblematic of Mrs Thatcher's popular capitalism, was also at the centre of this shift in our welfare state. The huge popularity of the policy – and the decision not to replace homes that were sold – meant that 1.7m social housing units were taken out of circulation between 1981 and 1995.[23] Council housing began to shift from a public service to a residual safety net for the poor. The pattern was repeated across the welfare state. In social care, local authorities supplied more than two thirds of residential places for the elderly in 1974; 20 years later they provided less than a quarter.[24] In the welfare system, means-tested benefits were only 9% of the total in 1979-80; by 1995-96 they were 22%.[25] With the loss of this personal experience, many lost their affiliation to the welfare state. Support became vulnerable, reliant on a broader faith in the system's merit.

Faced with this inheritance, New Labour was torn between two strategies. One was universal benefits, designed to buy the middle classes into the system. The other was means testing, designed to focus resources on alleviating poverty. The way the circle was squared was through what the policy wonks called progressive universalism:[26] something for everyone, but more for those most in need. Child benefit, for example, had both a targeted element for poorer households and a universal element available to everyone.

That progressive universalism did not, on its own, address people's central concern: that others were not contributing to a shared system of insurance. Sometimes the system had the very opposite effect. The steady growth of means testing – the progressive part of progressive universalism – meant that to qualify for a range of benefits, you had to learn to either prove or perpetuate your poverty. Work too hard and your benefits would be withdrawn at the same time as taxes kicked in. For many, flipping burgers for a few extra pounds a week barely seemed worthwhile, leaving the benefits system complicit in – though not entirely to blame for – the rise of a workless class.

The sense of injustice this created was often at its most heightened around housing, where a focus on need, to the exclusion of contribution, has both ghettoised the workless class and frustrated those putting into the system. This was the story of Eric, a 40-year-old father of four who walked through the door of my constituency surgery shortly before the general election in 2010. He sat down in front of me while I read the summary taken by my caseworker. "Overcrowding. Four children. Six people in two-bedroom flat. In work. Told by council not enough points to move into somewhere bigger." It was a variation on the commonest theme at my constituency surgeries and also the most frustrating. I looked up at Eric and his plastic bag bristling with correspondence.

Taking this as his cue, he began to explain his situation. His family's flat had three rooms, but only because one of its large Edwardian rooms had been partitioned with plywood. The bed would not even fit in one of the resulting subdivisions, leaving his children sleeping on mattresses on the floor. The kids, he continued, had nowhere to do their homework, let alone play or have any privacy. The school had written to him saying that they were becoming increasingly disruptive in class, seemingly incapable of concentrating on what they were supposed to be doing. As his grievance came alive, tears began to flow.

Eric's story was, first and foremost, a reminder of one of Labour's biggest derelictions of duty in government: the failure to build, or facilitate the building of, enough homes that were fit for people to live in. It is a deficit unlikely to be remedied in the near future while another – the fiscal one – overrides all other considerations. But the result of this shortage has been to raise the stakes on how scarce housing is allocated. One in 12 Britons is on the social housing waiting list,[27] so the way that housing is allocated has a profound effect on many people's experience of the welfare state.

After the war, social housing was built not just for the working classes, but for the "general need" of society. Many of the postwar estates began life with a strong social mix and were seen as desirable places to live. As late as 1979, 20% of the richest segment of the population lived in social housing.[28] This was soon to change. "Right to buy" allowed tenants to purchase their own homes at discounted rates but prevented councils from using the proceeds to invest in new ones. A shrinking council housing stock was prioritised to those most in need of housing. The result has been that deprivation and worklessness are now concentrated on those estates. Today if you live on an estate and have two people of working age as your neighbours, the chances of them both working are just one in 10.[29]

The effect has been deeply detrimental. Adults living in council housing are often outside the social networks that bring about job opportunities, with only half of all jobs advertised at job centres.[30] Long-term unemployment contributes to problems with depression, alcohol and drug addiction, which in turn make it harder for people to find work. Children grow up in communities where it has become normal not to work and go to schools that lack the social mix that most successful institutions enjoy. All too often low expectations follow.

For people like Eric, meanwhile, the system has been rewarding the wrong behaviour. The consequence of stripping out the "contributions" that Beveridge talked of, to focus exclusively on assessments of need, has been to alienate those who have worked hard. Many like him, who have struggled on with low pay despite the barriers set up by the benefit system, feel they have been punished for doing the right thing. These are the frustrations that bubbled over following the riots. People were already angry at a system they felt had grown lopsided. From their perspective, a system built on give and take had been reduced to one where many give while others take. Reciprocity had been swapped for charity; solidarity for resentment.

Affordable ownership

When some of those benefiting from that charity reduced homes to ashes and turned high streets into war zones, we reached a tipping point. People were not willing to countenance the idea that those who had behaved so selfishly should be living in homes subsidised by the society they had so little regard for. The sense of injustice was magnified when people considered their own situation. The average age of first-time buyers is creeping towards 40.[31] The average deposit required for a first home has risen from 16% of annual income in 1999 to 64% in 2009.[32] The financial crisis and the subsequent recession have forced many people to give up on their mortgages and re-enter the rental sector. The very idea of popular capitalism is on the brink of extinction. With council estates increasingly a reservoir for the workless poor, those who make a contribution to the welfare state, like Eric, feel abandoned by it when they need somewhere to live.

As well as increasing the supply of homes in order to gradually reduce prices, we must revisit the model to make ownership rapidly more affordable. The credit crunch revealed the folly of relying on reckless mortgage lending to people hoping to gain a foothold on the housing ladder. A new government is now about to prove the folly of selling over £9bn worth of land to the private sector without any planning requirements to build affordable homes on it.[33]

Rather than enable developers to build homes that will be out of reach for most people, the land should be transferred in trust to local communities. This model – the community land trust – has had stunning success in the US. The community retains ownership of the land, meaning people only have to find the money to buy the house itself. The community trust retains the right to buy back the house if the new owners prove anti-social neighbours. It also has the option of buying the house back at a fixed rate if the owners decide to move on, meaning that prices can be kept affordable for the next generation.[34] The model locks wealth into communities in a way that selling to private sector developers never could, giving people a stake not just in society in general but in their neighbourhoods in particular.

Not everyone will be able to afford to own a home, and with house prices still so high and low pay so prevalent, the need for more social housing has never been greater. But any new social housing must be seen to value contribution. In Manchester, the council rewards those who contribute to their community with higher priority on council waiting lists. If people have lived in the area, have a record of being in work and have done extra voluntary work to help others, they are given preference over others with similar levels of need. Of course councils have a responsibility to house those who would otherwise be homeless, but beyond this they should recognise the practical and ethical arguments for following Manchester's example.[35]

Where a tenant repeatedly breaks rules, or has been found guilty of involvement in criminality like the riots, the answer cannot be to simply evict them. This will only push people into the grasp of slum landlords or make them homeless. A better solution would be to make transgressors' continued tenancy conditional on their participation in intensive interventions. Trained professionals would be assigned to help them manage their lives, from making sure children are in school to requiring participation in drug and alcohol programmes where necessary.

Following the riots there is a grave danger of us cutting part of our society adrift. At a time in which the grotesques of Little Britain and Shameless saturate our culture, the temptation will be to lash out with a revival of punitive class politics. Just as the left once made the error of pitching the working class against the rest of society, today's government should resist the temptation to pitch the bulk of society against an ill-defined "underclass". The answer, instead, must be to rebuild a sense of reciprocity to knit society back together again. That means a working class with a stake in capitalism and a middle class with faith once again in the welfare state. It requires fulfilling the goals expressed by both Mrs Thatcher and Beveridge, not one or the other.

CHAPTER 3

NINE TO FIVE

Making work worthwhile

My father was a taxidermist – not a run-of-the-mill profession for a West Indian immigrant. As new arrivals in 1950s Britain looked for ways to make a living, few thought to stuff pet cats, mount deer heads on platters and arrange squirrels into frozen shapes. As with many immigrants, his original ambition had been thwarted by a lack of money, bureaucracy and straightforward discrimination. Having given up on becoming a vet, he settled for working with dead animals rather than live ones.

I spent countless Saturday and Sunday mornings roaming my father's factory, just south of the Spurs football stadium. It was a magical environment. A tour of the building would reveal painted glass eyes placed precisely in drawers and tusks, antlers, claws, teeth and skulls randomly stacked in corners. Giant skins of big cats – lions, tigers, leopards – were laid out like carpets, ready for mounting. Brown bottles of chemicals for tanning leather, with names that I couldn't pronounce and skulls and crossbones on the label, sat above on the shelves. Papier-mache mouldings stood paralysed on the wooden floorboards. Dad was a true craftsman, an artist. I remember watching his hands bring this menagerie to life, and his broad, bright-white-toothed smile when his array of customers – suited museum curators, Arab businessmen and local dog owners – walked out wearing satisfied expressions.

Many of my parents' West Indian contemporaries worked for British Rail, London Underground or the National Health Service, providing the backbone of Britain's infrastructure. These jobs hardly brought the excitement of my dad's jungle grotto but it was solid, dependable work, providing not just income but a sense of independence and pride.

As the 1980s loomed, the recession meant there was less money in the pockets of Dad's customers. The business phone stopped ringing quite so often. With a new agenda of animal rights, wildlife protection and licensing and export controls, he struggled to make a living. Our street, Dongola Road, had the Duke of Wellington pub at one end and William Hill at the other. As he worked less, he spent more time in both. He started drinking heavily. Once popular and jovial, he became something of a broken figure. As his business lost its way, so too did he.

'From the ashes'

Almost 30 years later I thought of my father as I walked, shell-shocked, down Tottenham High Road. Having been let through the police cordon to survey the damage the morning after Saturday night's riots, I headed slowly down the middle of the street, each footstep meeting with the crunch of broken glass, bricks and debris. On either side of the road were shopkeepers, returning to their stores for the first time since they had been robbed and ransacked.

After big football games in the 1980s, my dad would walk me along the same High Road with a bucket and spade. The police horses used frequently in those days to scatter inebriated football fans had usually left their own mark. I would trail alongside next to my father scooping up manure to take home for the compost heap. In 2011 the high street had the same eerily quiet feel to it, but the devastation surpassed anything that I remember seeing as a child.

As I passed the charred remains of two police cars and a double-decker bus, the full scale of the damage became clear. The fish-and-chip shop that fuelled my office during the general election campaign had had its windows smashed in. The opticians where I had bought my sunglasses only the summer before had been raided. The Carpetright shop that had provided the lino on my kitchen floor was barely recognisable after the damage done by arsonists. The post office where I had spent countless hours as a child queueing to cash my parents' child benefit cheque had been gutted by fire. There was the putrid smell of burning rubber and plastic emanating from the shell of the building.

Behind it was an even more bizarre and heartbreaking sight. A house stood cracked open after the fires the night before. Three walls were intact but one was missing entirely, with the roof open to the sky. Like a doll's house or the set of a theatre, you could see straight into the living room and upstairs bedroom. Picture frames were still on the walls. It would have looked less incongruous in an earthquake zone than on a London high street.

Many of the shopkeepers were in tears. Outside one newsagent, three Turkish men sat on plastic crates in stunned silence. The lady who runs Tottenham Travel was picking up the glass and brochures from the floor of her shop. One owner had a clipboard and pencil in his hands, counting up his lost stock. These were independent business owners, fiercely proud of what they had achieved. Their shops were monuments to years of hard graft. The night that had just passed was not only an attack on their property; it was an attack on their identity and sense of self-worth.

A few days later the television cameras were allowed through the cordon to cover the clean-up operation organised by the community. Camera crews and reporters clutching microphones hustled through to get their first glimpse of an area that had last been filmed from helicopters. One of those interviewed by the gaggle of journalists was Steve Moore, a local businessman. The owner of Paradise Gems, a jewellery shop on the High Road just two doors up from the post office, Steve has been in the trade for 32 years. Rioters had looted and then burned his shop to the ground. When I had spoken to him the morning after the riots he was caught between shock and devastation. Like everyone else, he saw no link between the loss of a man's life to a police bullet and the ransacking of his shop by gangs of youths.

Now he was looking forward. Shock had turned into a determination to get back on his feet. Standing in front of the film crews, he struck an incredible tone of defiance: "I've had over 25 robberies in my life. I've been stabbed, had a samurai through my leg twice and threatened with a gun… I've survived and I carry on. I want to carry on. To come back from the ashes."

Work gave him character, pride and purpose. It gave him a role in society in the same way as my father's business had once done for him. Despite what had been thrown at him, no one was going to take that away.

Character

The contrast with those who looted shops and burned down buildings could not have been starker.

If work is one of the things that provide us with a character – a role to play in society – then its prolonged absence can be deeply corrosive to our sense of who we are and what we stand for. I saw in my father what happens when days are not structured around anything productive, but characterised by drift, boredom and despair. Long-term unemployment, when you could be working, saps not just your skills but your self-respect. Many of those who looted had become demoralised in a literal sense – detached from the norms and codes shared by the rest of society.

Three of the areas worst affected by the riots – Haringey, Hackney and Lewisham – are the three places with the highest levels of unemployment in England.[1] In Haringey, more than 10,000 people were out of work at the time of the riots, fighting it out for only 367 vacancies.[2] In Hackney there were fewer than 500 vacancies for 11,000 claimants.[3] In riot-hit Wolverhampton close to one in three 16- to 24-year-olds can't find work.[4] In Birmingham, in the month of the riots, over 4,000 people in that age group had been unemployed for more than six months.[5]

Some of this can be blamed on the credit crunch. The number of long-term jobless doubled in the period between the credit crunch and the riots[6] but we should not kid ourselves that this is a phenomenon of the past three years alone. Despite historically low levels of unemployment in the years prior to the crash, there still are almost 300,000 households where no one has ever worked.[7] A quarter of a million children live in these homes,[8] growing up believing that it is not normal to get up each morning to go to work. This didn't happen overnight.

Before I left for America to study and then practise law in the mid-1990s, more than 12,500 people were unemployed in Tottenham alone, well over a quarter of those of working age.[9] The recession of the early 1990s had hit N17 hard – more so than those of the previous decade. High interest rates had crippled many families with debt. People weren't spending and the service industries – the staples of employment in the area – were shrinking. There were no jobs available, no serious government programmes to help people learn new skills or stay in touch with working life. I left with memories of men sitting outside the Swan pub drinking from morning until late at night.

Three years later, I returned to an economy restored to growth, but the men were still there. The same men drinking in the same pub, still out of work. Over a decade later, now as their MP, I've watched how they've slowly made the transition from the dole queue to the in-patients clinic. Many suffer from an array of mental health problems, from alcoholism to depression, that can be traced back to their prolonged period out of work. Now their children are at the start of the same journey.

The system that was supposed to help these families has become part of the problem. A series of means tests, designed to divert resources towards the least well off, has made it increasingly difficult for people to work their way out of poverty. Those entering work have faced the double whammy of benefits being withdrawn and income taxes kicking in, both at the same time. The result is that some have found themselves taking home very little extra from their new pay packets. At worst, people have kept only five or 10 pence in every pound they have earned.[10]

Some have struggled on regardless, working hard for very little reward – in Britain today over half of poor children live in a working household[11] – but others have opted out of work entirely. The results have been catastrophic, for both taxpayers and those in perpetual receipt of benefits. Those putting into a system of national insurance have felt cheated by others treating welfare as a choice rather than an insurance policy. Meanwhile, those on benefits for long periods have seen their own chances of any sort of career slip away.

Making work pay

The coalition government has promised to simplify the benefits system. In theory, at least, there should be broad support for any plan that prevents people from getting lost in a maze of bureaucracy. But the danger is that the reforms will not do enough to address the defects of the old system. Under the government's plans one in five low earners will still have a marginal tax rate of 50%[12] – losing half of every extra pound earned as benefits are deducted and taxes kick in. As a country we risk repeating some of the mistakes of the past. Work will still feel barely worthwhile for many. If the system can be simplified further, at reasonable cost, then it should be.

In the long term, the goal should be to merge the tax and benefit systems completely. The plethora of benefits would be replaced with a single simple system. A line would be drawn at an agreed level of income for a family. Those families with incomes above the line would begin to pay taxes; those below the line would be recipients of tax credits but not be taxpayers themselves. No one would pay tax and receive benefits at the same time, with all the complexity and perverse incentives that brings. Without countless means tests, people would not have the indignity of having to repeatedly prove their poverty, nor would there be the uncertainty about whether work would bring in more money than benefits. On the left some call this a national minimum income; on the right it is described as a negative income tax. The labels matter far less than the principle: that a far simpler system should protect those who lose their jobs, and make working worthwhile again.

Meanwhile, people must be reassured that others will put into the system, not just take out. Many of those who took part in the riots have never been fully acquainted with the rigours and the fulfilment of proper work. Government should step in after a year of unemployment to stop the rot. We should put people to work in the public and voluntary sectors rather than pay them to sit at home. Work placements should last for up to six months and be no more than 30 hours a week, to allow people time to search for more permanent jobs.[13] People should be guaranteed a job on a decent wage – and required to either take it or forgo their benefits.

To cover the costs of these measures, the tax system ought to focus more on unearned wealth acquired through speculation, and less on the income produced by genuine enterprise and hard work. The financial crisis exposed the fallacy that we can all become richer simply from trading the same stock of houses.[14] There were certainly winners and losers from the merry-go-round – for example, when the Jubilee line was extended on the London Underground, property values near its stations rose by £2.8bn in Southwark and Canary Wharf alone.[15] But much of this wealth was not earned in the true sense – by creating great new products and much-needed jobs.

Meanwhile, the bankers who financed many of these mortgages got rich through privatising profits but socialising their losses. It is this kind of accumulation of unearned wealth, in the City and in the housing market, that should be the target for the taxman, not the hard work of shop owners and their employees on Tottenham High Road.

Spitting on your onion rings

We should be honest with ourselves, though. The work that really builds character – the character that the rioters so patently lacked – comes from jobs that are themselves rewarding in every sense: jobs that contribute to personal growth as well as economic growth, jobs that give you a stake in society, not just poverty wages and something to do on weekdays. A job without these things may be bearable for a few months, but it is no life.

Few of the looters who were in work had respected jobs to jeopardise with a criminal record. The exceptions, including a former Olympic ambassador,[16] made the news precisely because they were exceptional. It was those with little to lose and little to be proud of who helped themselves to the consumer goods they foolishly thought would afford them status.

Previous generations were willing to soldier on in roles that came with little pay and even less respect. Certainly my parents had no qualms about which jobs they took up when they arrived in Britain – anything would do. As I grew up, I graduated from paper rounds during the school holidays to spells behind the counter in fast-food chains while at university. I still feel oddly nostalgic when I pass the old site of KFC in Tottenham. It takes me back to the customers who place orders without looking at you, the name badge that you don't want to wear, and the starchy uniform trousers with their pockets sewn up so that money from the till can't walk out of the door.

Today's youths have other ideas. They grow up in a culture in which Eminem mocks spotty kids "working at Burger King spitting on your onion rings". To work hard for low wages in a uniform that you hate is seen as naive, not sensible or dignified.

The business of business

The problem is that politics is unable to speak to any of this. Successive governments have lost touch entirely with the idea of a good working day.

Everyone likes the idea of good work in theory but the problem is that our political leaders think it is none of their business. The assumption is that the private sector is just that: private. Bold statements by our leaders about freedom, equality, happiness and empowerment come with their own small print: not applicable on weekdays between the hours of nine and five.

This assumption can be traced back to the liberal economic revolution of the 1980s. With socialism defeated, free marketers insisted that companies should be liberated to pursue their own ends. The logic was simple: shareholders own companies; only they can decide what a company is for. Governments should refrain from interfering; the employees' job is to maximise the returns to shareholders. As Milton Friedman, a Nobel economist and guru of Mrs Thatcher, put it, "There is one and only one social responsibility of business – to use its resources and engage in activities designed to increase its profits."[17] The business of business is business. Compassion and humanity can be reserved for public services.

In government New Labour never challenged this idea with any confidence. Instead, bad jobs were simply edited out of the official story about the British economy. The idea took hold that Britain would become a "knowledge economy". Low-skilled work would vanish overseas, leaving only those jobs that were highly skilled, highly paid and highly rewarding. As one government advisor put it in his bestselling book, "We are all in the thin-air business these days. In the past people made their living by extracting ore, mining coal, making steel, manufacturing cars, bringing cattle to market... These days most people in most advanced economies produce nothing that can be weighed: communications, software, advertising, financial services. They trade, write, design, talk, spin and create."[18]

As with so many exaggerations, the story has its roots in a real insight. The number of jobs available to people without qualifications has been falling for a decade;[19] there is a good chance that your dishwasher was made in China but designed in Britain.

But the "new economy" is an exaggeration. The fastest-growing occupations in modern Britain are in low-paid areas like data input and administration.[20] Cafes can't relocate to Beijing. Hotels can't move to Mumbai. Gyms, swimming pools and parking lots aren't going anywhere. Someone still needs to drive the bus, take your coat in a cloakroom or collect your rubbish once a week. These are not industries that have had to respond to global competition; there is no stampede to train staff up and double everyone's wages. Over four million of us are dissatisfied or very dissatisfied with our jobs,[21] while the worst-paying positions are still the least secure,[22] the least likely to provide training and advancement[23] and the least likely to offer any sense of personal satisfaction. As consumers we may be king, but step the other side of the counter and we are expected to behave like robots.

Good work

The ingredients for a good job are not complicated: a sense that you are respected and a fair share of the profits you help create. If the workforce had been listened to at KFC, perhaps we might have had trousers with pockets in, or shift patterns that were more convenient, or a chance to ditch the name badges we all hated. If we had been given a fairer share of the profits, perhaps I would have lasted more than a few weeks in the job. Perhaps now jobs flipping burgers would not be ridiculed in popular culture or judged quite so dispensable by would-be looters.

Elsewhere, these ideas are not so abstract. In Germany employees are represented on all company boards, encouraging employers to consider the interests of their staff and vice versa.[24] Workers are listened to but they are also expected to take responsibility for the success of the firm. The result has not been stagnation but a dynamism that should make us envious: Germany has been more productive than Britain for two decades now.[25]

In France, employees in companies with more than 50 workers are obliged to offer their employees a share in their profits over and above their wages.[26] We could do the same here. Any profits that exceed a set threshold would be shared 50:50 between shareholders and employees, giving employees a real stake in the success of the firm. Employees' profits would be invested in company shares, held in trust along the lines of the John Lewis model, so that collectively employees would build up a real stake in the company that they work for.

These two changes – sharing power and sharing profits – could bring about a fundamental shift in the types of jobs on offer, helping narrow the gap between the so-called 'lovely' and 'lousy' jobs in modern Britain. They ought also to command cross-party support. In some ways both ideas chime with David Cameron's "big society". They stem from the recognition that governments are good at setting minimum standards and basic entitlements, but only so much can be mandated from Whitehall. Their focus is not on red tape but on conversations and relationships in every workplace.

The problem is that they won't happen. Like others before him, the prime minister is prepared to be a radical reformer only within the strict confines of public services. The flaw in the big society is that it is not big enough to reach beyond the public sector. There are promises to promote mutual business models – but only in the public sector. The rest of the economy is still considered beyond the remit of politics. The economic revolution of the 1980s casts a long shadow and the present government shows no sign of stepping out from it. This spells bad news for Britain because work matters not just for our economy, but also for the character of our society.

CHAPTER 4

BOYS' NIGHT OUT

Why young men go bad

Each tragedy has at least one image that sums it up. The riots of August 2011 had several. The picture of the woman jumping from a burning building in Croydon looked unnervingly like something from a war zone. Images of looters trying on clothes before stealing them captured the surreal, disturbing ease with which some made the transition to criminality. The picture of Tariq Jahan bravely coming to terms with the death of his son stands out as an oasis of humanity amid the violence and the anger.

The images of the rioters themselves were less shocking. Young angry men in tracksuits, hooded tops and face masks: these were the all-too-familiar lead characters in a drama broadcast around the world.

Perhaps because we've got so used to this particular type of hoodlum, we have lost the appetite to ask why they are who they are. Of all the statistics to emerge, the fact that 91% of those arrested were male[1] has been almost completely overlooked. Imagine if nine out of 10 rioters had been female. The media would be awash with gender specialists discussing a crisis in femininity. When it is men terrorising neighbourhoods, burning down homes and clashing with the police, the response is a shrug of the shoulders: "Boys will be boys."

Britain has trouble with boys. In our schools, they are slipping behind girls as early as the age of five, with 53% reaching the expected level in writing compared with 72% of girls.[2] Boys are three and a half times more likely to be permanently excluded from school,[3] while men account for 95% of the prison population. [4] Boys and young men are struggling to find their place in society. We must start asking ourselves why.

Without a full public inquiry, setting out who the rioters were, we will never know just how many of those who were implicated in the riots – old and young – grew up without a male role model in their home. But there are some things we do know. Of the 19 local boys arrested during the riots in Tottenham, 14 were already known to the local authority's youth offending service. Only two lived in households where both parents were present.[5]

Some will end up in Feltham young offenders' institution. On my last visit, a prison officer told me that in his five years there he had seen only two fathers come to visit. The boys have usually grown up without positive male role models, adopting the warped versions of masculinity projected in popular culture. They don't want to wear a suit or carry the toolbox of an artisan; they want the baggy jeans, the bling and the women from the grime videos.

Theirs is the world of the alpha male, where "respect" is everything. Look at someone the wrong way, or stray into the wrong postcode, and you could lose your life. Carry a knife or a gun and you are a real man. Become a "baby-father", have children with a string of different women, and people will look up to you. No one ever taught these boys that the inability to delay gratification, the obsession with status symbols and a worldview centred on the self are markers not of manhood, but of immaturity.

A short goodbye

My most enduring memory of my own father was being pulled towards him as we stood on platform five at Kings Cross station. Hugging me close and kissing my ear, he whispered, "Take care of Mum, OK?" He was leaving the next day for the United States. Aged 12, I was returning to boarding school in Peterborough. I never saw him again.

Life in our family home had been far from idyllic. Things were going badly in my parents' marriage. Dad was drinking heavily, jobless and gambling. Mum seemed to peck at him endlessly, raging at his pathetic condition. They argued about the same things over and over, having the same unresolvable conversations that had taken place hundreds of times before.

With Britain's inner cities hit badly by the recessions of the 1980s, many West Indians who had migrated to England 30 years earlier continued their journey onward to Canada and the US. For my father, America held out the promise of a fresh start. For my siblings and me, it meant life with one parent rather than two.

In Tottenham, most families were more subject to economic currents than able to chart their own course. If you wanted more than low-level, low-paid work, between bouts of prolonged unemployment, you had to get out. Opportunity was elsewhere. People drifted away for their own reasons. The common theme was that families struggled to be families. The relationships didn't hold. Never mind community breakdown; even the most fundamental social relationship could not stand up to the economic tides.

In Peterborough, where I had won a choral scholarship, things were different. There, I was far more self-conscious about the stigma surrounding our family. Why did I have one parent, not two, sitting next to me at parents' evening? Why was only my mum watching me in the school play? Why was it that everybody else had a father shouting their name on sports day? The only other person at the school that I remember with only one parent was a classmate whose father had been killed in action during the Falklands war.

Although I made friends and found kind and generous teachers, there were many moments when I struggled to cope with what felt like betrayal by my father. My initial anxieties were predictable: when the first hint of stubble appeared on my face, who would teach me how to shave? When I was called "queer" because I didn't make it into the first rugby team at school, who was going to tell me whether to fight back or walk away? Each Christmas morning I felt the same disappointment. Fathers' Day loomed liked an annual ordeal.

More problematic were the frustrations that came with being back in Tottenham. I was surrounded by friends and a community that rightly felt the world was stacked against them. I would exchange stories with black friends who had been turned down for jobs, or told to keep away from people's daughters, because they had the wrong name, skin tone or postcode. The lure of urban street culture would grow stronger. The messages from rap and hip-hop lyrics would hit home harder. The anger, the sense of injustice and the temptation to lash out would grow and grow – and I missed out on having a father who would set me straight.

Without her husband, my mother fought desperately hard to hold her family together, reaching deep into a formative black cultural experience that relied heavily on faith and self-help. My siblings and I would be at church on a Sunday, perfectly turned out, whether we liked it or not. Mum believed in God but, like many folk in Tottenham, she also took solace in the sense of fellowship surrounding our church. Faith was a reason for her children to shun some of the tempting shortcuts offered by street culture and drugs.

Mum worked non-stop, doing two, sometimes three, jobs throughout the 80s. Days would be spent as a home help for the infirm and disabled, evenings and weekends as a care assistant in an old people's home. In her spare time, she sold Tupperware door to door. Naturally shy and with no formal education after the age of 15, Mum relied heavily on me and my siblings to help her navigate the reams of bureaucracy that my father had previously handled. The mortgage, insurance, passport applications and school letters were all a communal effort. My mother's was a traditional West Indian conservatism, brought with her from the calm of rural Guyana to the chaos of urban London. It was her way of keeping her family intact in a world of financial pressures, disruptive commercial influences and social unrest.

For traditionalists, single parents were totemic. They chose to ignore the fact that most were abandoned by their partners as opposed to being the victims of their own "promiscuity". As commentators and politicians lambasted the assumed moral failings of single mothers, I came to appreciate the voices who wanted to stand up for people like my mother – smart, dedicated and deserted by her husband. They came overwhelmingly from liberals in the Labour party and beyond, who realised that women like her were performing heroics and needed help, not insults. Ours may not have been a classically liberal household but one thing was clear: when it mattered, the liberal left was on our side.

Dads

The danger is that those same liberals who fought so hard for single mothers like mine now give the impression that fatherlessness does not matter at all. Some, though by no means all, choose to dismiss the importance of family structure altogether. They insist that it is the quality of parenting, not the quantity of parents, that matters, that the loss of a father only really matters if it means a loss of income, that all the talk of role models is overblown pop psychology. That's not how I remember it.

After the riots, I am even more convinced about the importance of fatherhood. We can no longer afford for fathers to either opt out of or be shut out of family life. In particular, two dysfunctional models of fatherhood need to be addressed: the absent father and the disengaged father.

The implication of this is not that government should waste millions on a tax break for married couples that failed utterly in the 1980s, when marriage rates declined throughout the decade.[6] It is that fathers must be held properly to account.

For too long the absent father has been given an easy ride, permitted to walk away from his responsibilities by weak legislation and a hapless Child Support Agency (CSA). That mistake is being repeated under this government, which has chosen to punish women rather than support them when they are left with a child.

Under new legislation, single mothers will be asked to pay for the CSA to collect the money they are owed. Not only will the CSA charge an initial fee of £100 – no small sum for many women left on their own – but the agency will charge a commission of between 7% and 12% on whatever is collected.[7]

Women head 90% of the single-parent families in Britain.[8] It is women who will foot the bill. The state should be a living embodiment of our responsibilities towards one another, not a glorified debt collector hacking off its own slice of the profits. The government should be making it easier, not harder, for women to chase down errant fathers. Those who walk away from their children, imagining that they can divorce a child in the same way one might a partner, should have money taken directly from their salaries or benefits.

There is much, much more to being a father than paying money into a bank account once a month, but this is the very least we should expect. At present, only mothers are legally required to place their name on their child's birth certificate. Where the father is known, he should be obliged to register his name and National Insurance number on the certificate. If necessary this would allow any future child maintenance payments to be deducted at source from either wages or benefits.

Between a quarter and a third of children with separated parents have little or no contact with their father.[9] There are many fathers who are out of their child's life for a good reason but their prevalence should not be overstated – only one in six absent fathers is judged to present a significant problem for his children.[10] The remainder should continue to play a role in their offspring's lives when their relationship with the mother breaks down.

Even when the separated father wants to play a role, the state is inflexible and uncompromising. A third of UK children who were born to two parents in a relationship will see them separate before they turn 16.[11] Making support available to separating couples to ensure relationships remain civil is a first step. More often than not, the children are left in the primary care of their mother. Too often the father is then written out of the story altogether, as schools and GPs pass information on to just the one parent. This leaves too many fathers reliant on secondhand information and denied the chance to play an active role in their children's education or health. Similarly, when the father leaves the family home, the state gives no consideration to giving him housing that can accommodate his children. Rarely will a father feel comfortable having his kids stay the night in the bedsit he has been allocated. We must make sure that our public services are "father-proofed", so that the state does not come between a good father and his children.

Those fathers who are still with the mother of their children, meanwhile, should be given all the help they need. Society has undergone some historic changes over the past 50 years as women have entered the workforce in their millions. Over the past 60 years the number of mothers in employment has tripled.[12] Today, around two-thirds of mothers are in paid work.[13] Yet there has been no comparable revolution in the family home. Often it is still Mum who does the cooking, helps with the homework and reads bedtime stories. Dad is the one who creeps in the door each night when the kids are already in bed. Four in 10 fathers in Britain feel that they do not spend enough time with their children, a figure that rises to more than half for couples with children under one.[14]

In part the answers to this are cultural rather than political – a question of challenging outdated attitudes. Many men are still more comfortable in the provider-protector role, having grown up watching their own fathers act as the breadwinner and disciplinarian in the household. Changing attitudes comes first.

But the problem is also one that we perpetuate through the law. Many fathers want to be more involved but are never given the chance. Britain enjoys some of the highest levels of maternity leave in Europe, but among the lowest levels of paid paternity leave. This huge imbalance entrenches a particular model of the family – fathers can't afford to take time off work, making it much harder for couples to share the joys and the burdens of caring as well as earning. Women's pay and career progression, meanwhile, suffer while they take long stretches off.

If fathers really are to have a strong emotional bond with their children, it must start early. Britain should follow the lead of countries like Norway, where parental leave can be split between the mother and the father. One third of this leave should be reserved for mothers, one third for fathers and one third left open for couples to use as they choose. The move could help to revolutionise fatherhood and stop women being penalised at work for being the principal carer.

Role models

One of the most depressing features of the riots was the role models chosen by many of those involved. Breathless posts on social networking sites about "the Feds" betrayed pretensions among petty thieves to be American gangsters. There is an important lesson here about the role models available to boys outside the family when fathers are not around.

Growing up, I relied heavily on other figures around me, some real, some imagined. Teachers, priests and youth workers all helped fill the great father-shaped hole in my life, offering advice when I asked for it and a stern word where necessary. Almost as important were Sunday nights, when Bill Cosby would beam out of The Cosby Show as a sort of proxy father to relate to and laugh along with, worlds away though his world was.

I was fortunate to have an older brother to keep me level-headed throughout a turbulent adolescence. Others were less lucky. They found themselves being schooled by rappers and, in some cases, gang members. The result was that, much like the boys in Feltham prison today, they grew up with a twisted notion of what it meant to be a man.

Since my teenage years, many of the social structures that I relied upon have begun to wane. Our neighbourhoods have become more atomised – we are less likely to know our neighbours or live near our relatives. In immigrant communities – like the black Caribbean community that I grew up among in Tottenham – the common identity of those first to arrive is fading among the third and fourth generations. Churches have less reach into communities than they once did.

As for schools, one in four primaries has no male teacher.[15] Young boys can still grow up without coming into meaningful contact with a working man.

Meanwhile, the subversive forces of gang culture are as strong as ever. Twenty years ago, Ice Cube was telling my generation of inner city boys, "I got a shotgun, and here's the plot / Takin niggaz out with a flurry of buckshots... life ain't nothin' but bitches and money." Today, Giggs is telling young men, "And I don't care if I ain't got a strap on me / If I got a knife, im' a push apart skin... I got no time to put my sperm in a bitch" to a beat punctuated by a cacophony of gunshots.[16] For most boys these lyrics are just entertainment, but for boys with little else to teach them how to express their masculinity, the result can be toxic.

Just as I used to see some of my old school friends spiral into anger and violence in an attempt to mimic the words of NWA, I watch the same happen to my young constituents as they try to ape artists like Giggs. The amateur music videos they post on YouTube demonstrate a flair for music but also a destructive, nihilistic worldview. "Make money, take money / And when it ain't working out, run up in a nigga's crib and take that money, take that money" is the chorus of one. The protagonist is shown cruising around a Tottenham housing estate, holding up his gold chain while children who look no older than eight or nine make gun signs into the camera.

This video features the Northumberland Park Killers (NPK), one of 12 gangs active in and around Tottenham, and one of well over 100 in London alone.[17] While some gangs in Britain are sophisticated machines involved in drug trafficking and racketeering, the vast majority are just like the NPK: street gangs tussling for turf. The NPK, based near the Tottenham Hotspur football ground, battle the Shankstarz, based in Silver Street in Edmonton. This is N17 versus N18. What drives them is pride, not economics.

The pain is not confined to their own world. Etched into my memory are the events of a night in 2005 where I saw a young man shot down outside the Broadwater Farm Community Centre. He and I had been there for the

Ghanaian Community Education Awards. Minutes earlier I had presented him with a prize for his outstanding school results. He was now fighting for his life after being shot from a passing car as he was leaving.[18] He was no gangster, but the men in the car didn't know or care about that. They were from the Wood Green Mob in neighbouring N22 and wanted to make a statement by shooting someone on rival turf.

Gang life has bastardised their notion of civic pride by dictating that they will always be at war. They will always need to threaten violence, if not employ it. They are told they must kill or be killed. Their pride has morphed into paranoia: they live in fear of what lies beyond what they know. It limits their world to the boundaries of a housing estate. I have met countless boys and young men who cannot remember the last time they left Haringey. Their lives are needlessly parochial. They have no idea of the opportunities that lie elsewhere in London, let alone in the rest of the country.

It remains to be seen what role individual gangs played in orchestrating the riots in England. But what is crystal clear is that the culture that gangs cultivate was the engine of the unrest. A willingness to employ violence, a disrespect for the life and property of innocent others and a take-what-you-can attitude were laid bare for all to see. This cannot be viewed as simply the phenomenon of material poverty. You cannot wish it away with extra tax credits or by giving a youth centre a lick of paint. This is about broadening horizons. It is about restoring a healthy relationship with the rest of society.

Mentors

We have to get serious about giving inner city boys other role models to learn from. So far, our engagement with them has not stretched beyond small-scale projects. Sports programmes and anti-knife crime campaigns are valuable, but ultimately treat the symptoms and not the disease. In London, the Mayor's Fund is an honourable attempt to harness the wealth of the business community to improve young lives, but it misses something important. There is more to philanthropy than finance. Young men in inner cities need access to powerful role models in person, not just their chequebooks.

Young men need to see what hard work can deliver. They need to be able to conceive of an existence where being a man is not about looking tough, but about being able to translate your talents into success. What a difference it would make if the same philanthropists who write generous cheques could be equally forthcoming with their time, if they could impart something far more valuable than money: ambition. Many City firms already commit their staff to as many as three days a year of what they term "corporate social responsibility" but this might involve nothing more than repainting a school fence. More fulfilling – for both the students and the workers – would be a proper, sustained mentoring relationship.

In Kent County, Michigan, a state blighted by some of the worst urban poverty in America, schemes help local businesses offer discounts to people who volunteer as mentors. In the UK, our ambition should be to replicate these ideas on a much bigger scale. The government should explore what incentives it can offer firms to have their staff mentoring kids from the inner city. League tables could be published every year – for example setting out which firms have donated the most hours, not just money, to mentoring young people from tough backgrounds. The government might even offer some financial reward, like a tax rebate, for the most time-generous firms in each area. This might motivate bosses to help their staff do their bit.

Becoming a man is a turbulent process at the best of times. There are bouts of insecurity, reinvention and fragility. The angry young men in the riots had been lost to a nihilistic subculture long ago because they had no one to steer them through their journey to manhood. A good father can never be replaced fully. But the very least government and society can do together is to help soften the blow.

Saying goodbye

As for my own father, he never found a way to be part of my day-to-day life again. Only when I became an MP in 2000 did we speak briefly on the phone. I had tracked him down to Texas. I had learned that he was poor and drinking heavily, but on the phone his voice was full of emotion, and I savoured his words: "I knew you'd do it; I knew you'd do it." Three years later, he suddenly fell seriously ill. The news opened old wounds. I went back and forth over whether I should visit Dad in his last months. I decided to stay. I had only been an MP for a couple of years and wasn't ready to open the Pandora's box I'd kept closed for 18 years. A few months later, on 13 February 2003, my father died, leaving me to face the finality of my decisions and his.

It wasn't until 18 months had passed that I felt ready to bring some closure to our relationship. On a visit to the States, I decided to head to my father's grave. My plan was to leave the airport, pay my respects and then catch a flight to Miami a few hours later for my journey home. As I walked out of the air-conditioned sanctity of the airport, a thick wall of heat struck me. I telephoned an uncle who lived in the US to get the exact location of my father's grave. We had a brief, uncomfortable conversation about my father's outstanding medical bills before he gave me the name of the graveyard where Dad was buried.

I jumped into a cab driven by an unassuming middle-aged Nigerian. Learning of the reason for my trip, he stopped the meter, introduced himself as Ade, and told me he would be my guide. As we talked, my nerves increased and I tried to hide my anxiety in flippancy. But Ade saw through me. "Pay your respects in good faith and honour the dead with dignity," he told me as he talked poignantly about his own father and village elders in his home country.

En route to the cemetery we passed through several poor black neighbourhoods. All seemed to be populated by overweight, shuffling people. This was not the dynamic, soulful, pulsating black America I knew from an exhilarating few years studying at Harvard and then practising as a lawyer. This was another America: broken, beaten and bowed. This was the America my father had lived in. After an hour or so, we drew into the cemetery. A vast plain, it backed onto a teeming freeway. At one end was a gas station; at the other, a tawdry hardware store. Endless tombstones lay higgledy-piggledy across the expanse. It was not a well-tended place. I struggled for about half an hour to find Dad's grave. Eventually I realised it was just a numbered plot. No tombstone, no flowers. Nothing. All that differentiated it from a mound of dirt was a small plaque marked "No. 224313". Dad had died a pauper, penniless and broken.

Tears welled in my eyes but I was unable to cry, unable to realise any attachment to the moment. What's in a life, I thought, staring at the dusty grass beneath my feet. As a cool breeze blew over me, I knelt down and whispered, "I forgive you." What more could I say? In a daze, I wandered towards the nearby gas station and bought some plastic flowers in a metal container. I plonked them in the ground in front of my father's plot before standing for a moment, staring blankly at the makeshift shrine. It was nothing much, but it was some sort of marker – not just for my father, but also for me.

Despite everything he put my mother through, and despite the way he shirked his responsibilities to our family, I had long before decided there was no point in bearing a grudge against my dad. I like to think of him not as an inherently bad man, but as someone who lost his confidence, his self-respect and his way. He is a constant reminder to me of the sad spiral of destruction that can occur when a man loses sight of his purpose in life, and the devastating fallout borne by the family he leaves behind.

CHAPTER 5

LOOT

Why risk prison for a pair of trainers?

This was a surreal riot. What shocked was not just the violent clashes with the police – reminiscent of Toxteth and Brixton in 1981, Broadwater Farm in 1985, Los Angeles in 1992 and Paris in 2005. The images, captured by CCTV, mobile phones, video cameras and film crews, relayed the sheer audacity of the looters. Riots in previous decades had involved looting, but never had we seen it in high definition like this. Some of the scenes were jaw-dropping: people trying on clothes before stealing them; thieves lining up politely to use detaggers, presumably considering queue-jumping beyond the pale; others turning up expectantly at shopping centres at daybreak, hours after the disturbances had started. The palpable sense that "everything must go".

As the first night of the riots wore on, the range of those involved diversified. BlackBerry messages, texts and tweets spread across north London with news of the lawlessness.

There are even suggestions that rival gangs from outside the area put aside their differences to join in the melee in N17. These new arrivals were not only interested in the casual destruction of a neighbourhood; they were also drawn by the rich pickings. In neighbouring Wood Green mobile phone shops came under attack. But it wasn't until later in the night that the most serious incidents of looting took place.

As the police slowly regained control of Tottenham High Road, they pushed youths into the side streets that lead to Tottenham Hale. The Hale area sits in the south-east of Tottenham and is dominated by the train station that many will have passed through en route to Stansted airport. The high footfall that comes with such a transport hub made the area the ideal location for a sizeable retail park. Now this became the site for a buy-now-don't-pay-later free-for-all that continued well into the next day.

With the High Road suffering the most damage, I spent most of the aftermath there. It was only a few weeks later that I was able to make a proper visit to the retail centre. I had detected little sympathy for the retail giants in either Tottenham or Westminster. Many felt that these corporations could easily absorb any losses that weren't already covered by their insurance. That Peter Cowgill, the chairman of JD Sports, appeared on the radio to light-heartedly dismiss the riots as "proof that demand is strong" seemed to confirm that belief.

Visiting the stores themselves revealed the human cost. The managers in the retail park are fiercely proud of what they do. Some have worked their way up from summer jobs on the shop floor to run outlets that turn over upwards of a million pounds a month. On my visit their voices were laced with anger as they told me of the damage done on the night of the looting.

One such manager was Barry, who worked at the Comet at the southern end of the park between Lidl and Staples. A tall, middle-aged man, he was impressively eloquent. I began talking about the financial implications, asking how much stock had been stolen and how many trading hours had been lost, but that was not his primary concern. "What people forget is that my staff and I were the ones in here for days afterwards clearing up the mess," he said. Of course the financial loss mattered to him, but so too did the sense that others had such little regard for him or his staff.

It was not simply that every TV in the store had gone; it was that when he and his staff arrived at work the following morning, looting was still taking place in broad daylight. By that stage, it was more than the mob from the High Road ransacking the retail park – others had spotted the chance to pick up a new DVD player or Xbox or Sat Nav. An impromptu market had started up on Broad Lane as some came to buy goods barely metres from where they had been stolen. He pointed me towards some of the CCTV footage: so audacious had the looting become that after a while the thieves didn't even bother to cover their faces. They turned up in front of TV cameras and took whatever they could carry, leaving as if this were a completely normal shopping trip.

In the days that followed, the looting spread to Birmingham, Liverpool, Manchester and Bristol. In Tottenham Hale, the criminals returned to admire their handiwork. Some laughed while taking photographs of shop workers picking up the pieces. When the stores reopened, some even taunted employees that they would come back to resume the looting that very night. Barry recalled two people asking about a particular type of computer, only to boast that they had stolen one the week before. There was no shame in their actions, just pride in their new possessions. This was not a protest; it was rampant materialism.

There is always a temptation to explain away theft in such instances as one of the final acts of desperation. These were for the most part poor people, from depressed areas with a shrinking job market. Perhaps they had little choice but to steal? Such an argument is appealing to those inclined to examine the bigger picture, but it is also an insult to the countless others in those neighbourhoods who stayed in their homes, rather than taking to the streets. Besides, those who clambered through smashed shopfronts were not stealing bread, milk and butter to fill their stomachs, but simply taking the consumer goods that they coveted. You don't try things on if you are intending to sell them on. You don't ask how to work a computer unless you are planning on keeping it. All told, JD Sports alone had £700,000 worth of stock stolen – the equivalent of 20,000 pairs of trainers.[1] What was revealing was how much people valued what they were taking. How can a £35 pair of shoes ever be worth the risk of a criminal record and six months in prison?

'Reassuringly expensive'

I never resorted to theft but I remember the urgent "need" for new trainers. In my youth it was Nike Air Jordans, as worn by basketball legend Michael Jordan. His red and black trainers broke the mould – and the rules for a player's attire in the NBA. When the league tried to ban them for being the wrong colour, Jordan simply carried on wearing them, picking up a $5,000 fine every time he appeared on the court. Nike, of course, paid the fines and the publicity was enormous. I didn't play basketball. I didn't even watch it. But, like everyone else, I wanted a pair of Air Jordans.

Nike was one of the first companies to understand the emergence of a new youth culture, exported via the airwaves from the United States. What it picked up on – soon followed by others – was a spirit of individualism. We were a new generation growing up in a much more free-thinking Britain, where people were much less willing to conform to social norms and expectations. Not for us our parents' acceptance that identity should be determined by race or social class. This applied to me as much as anyone, having been transported from one world to another, Tottenham to Peterborough, via an Inter-City train ride. I didn't want to be "seen but not heard"; I wanted Nike Air Jordans!

For many of my mother's generation, a brand was reassurance, a promise of quality. For her in particular, coming from rural Guyana, where food was produced locally, brands were one way to negotiate the more anonymous world of supermarket chains and pre-packaged food. Spam was a regular, if unappetising, feature at mealtimes. Tinned fruit was served at birthday parties. Pot Noodles were stock-piled in our kitchen cupboards because Mum regarded processed food, made by the "experts", as a sign of quality. For me and my friends things were different. Retail, fashion and the service industry all sought to provide people with experiences, not just products. Perhaps more than any generation before, we grew up in an age where consumption and identity formed an intimate union.

The problem is that we can never have enough. The revolutions that have shaped modern Britain – the social liberalism of the 1960s and the economic liberalism of the 1980s – have schooled us to think of ourselves as individuals living lives free from each other. We like to believe that we each shape our own future, create our own identity and make our own choices. But the reality is that we are social animals, influenced by social emotions like pride and shame. We make choices based not just on our own preferences, but on the perceptions and judgments of others. The desire for the right pair of trainers or mobile phone is a question of keeping up with the Joneses.[2]

The advertising gurus worked this out long ago. There is a reason that Saab describes its vehicles as "anything but ordinary", that Maserati asks "What price exclusivity?", that Samsung invites us to "imagine the envy" should we buy one of its sleek new mobile phones.[3] Each of these adverts is about social status as well as personal preference. They rest on the understanding that a bigger house doesn't just provide more space to live in; it reassures us that we are moving up in the world. A faster car doesn't just get us to work quicker; it reveals to others how much we earn. The size of the rock on an engagement ring sends a message about the wealth and power of someone's would-be spouse. We buy these things to achieve status, admiration or respect.

While I sported Nike Air Jordans as a youth, scores of City traders began adopting pinstripe suits and wide braces. Many were self-consciously mimicking Gordon Gecko, the fictional character in Wall Street who became a cultural icon for his unashamed declaration, "Greed is good." The garish clothes were the City boys' two fingers to the criticism being levelled at them, in a culture where material possessions became signifiers of social status.

As Mrs Thatcher's dream of an enterprising Britain, underpinned by thrift and hard work, degenerated into something much more shallow and materialistic, writers and performers began to offer their own commentary on the times. Harry Enfield made his name mocking the new "loadsamoney" culture. "Excuse me, sport," one of his characters would say in a thick brummie accent. "I hope you don't mind me interrupting, only the wife and I noticed that we appear to be considerably richer than you." Next his wife would chip in: "Oh yes, we wear Chanel and Pierre Cardin, while our friends over here wear Next and C&A." "Oh yes," the triumphant businessman would conclude. "You get what you pay for and you earn what you're worth."

Take a walk today through the neighbourhoods where much of the looting took place and you will see some of the sacrifices people make to keep up with the competition. The bling on display – the gold rings, the big chains and expensive watches – is a defensive reaction against the indignity of poverty. Where a job or a house cannot convey status, expensive rims on a good car are pressed into service instead. People who live on the breadline still feel the pressure to wear the right brands and own the right phone. Parents in those areas find themselves working longer and longer hours so that they can buy their children the products they insist they need. Britain now has among the longest working hours in Europe.[4]

Where wages won't do the job, debt fills the void. When the financial crisis struck, Britain had the highest level of personal debt on record.[5] Four in 10 mortgages were being taken out not to buy homes, but rather for equity release, so that money could be spent rather than saved.[6] The promise of the consumer ethic is happiness, status and satisfaction, but with growing debt and longer working hours, stress and depression have rocketed. In 2008 more than 125,000 people went to see their GP about stress caused by debt.[7] Few of us want to give up the lifestyles that we have become accustomed to and that we see others enjoy.

Worst of all, a culture obsessed with "how to spend it" has produced a damaging indifference towards others. In the City, bankers have sold dodgy financial products to one another, concerned more about their end-of-year bonuses than about the consequences of such reckless risk-taking. In the inner city, the riots saw young men and women caught up in the urge to grab an iPhone or a home cinema at any cost to others. An impatient, materialistic culture breeds a take-what-you-can mentality. Colleagues, customers and strangers all become means to an end – people who either help us or hinder us in getting the things we want and are told we deserve.

To date, the response to a materialistic culture has been to push harder and harder for economic growth. But this has come at a real cost. Family policy has lost a sense of warmth and humanity, its focus turned almost exclusively to getting parents into work. Revolutionary programmes like SureStart have been scaled back to childminding services. Education policy has gone the same way, with a wide-ranging vision for lifelong learning soon reduced to a discussion about the economics of "human capital". The rhetoric has been about student choice, but the reality a much narrower concentration on science, technology, engineering and maths, often at the expense of the arts and humanities. Work has been instrumentalised as much as anything, with bad jobs seen as the price we pay to fund good consumer experiences. The idea that going to work might be a source of meaning, personal development and pride has barely figured. Arts and culture have enjoyed generous funding, but often on the basis that they will cut crime or prompt regeneration, rather than open minds or preserve our country's heritage.

The problem is that an expanding economy does not change the fundamental driver of materialism: the desire to keep up appearances. We spend more on our children's Christmas presents, but so do our neighbours. We buy a bigger house or a faster car, but so do our friends. We spend more and more on birthdays, weddings, stag and hen parties, and so does everyone else. What goes unchallenged is the basic idea that happiness is a commodity that can be bought and sold. We can shrink a discussion about materialism to a story of the "feral underclass" looting JD Sports for clothes "we" wouldn't be seen dead in. But the question for all of us is whether we can imagine a society and a culture that detach notions of social status from material possessions. Most of us would agree with the idea that there is more to life than money – but do we really mean it?

Culture and politics

We will not get there simply by passing a few laws. It is up to parents to take the lead, teaching their children that who you are is not determined by the brands you wear, that what you contribute matters as much as what you consume, that your worth isn't the same as your bank balance. Leaders from within communities, from teachers and youth workers to church pastors and imams, need to reinforce the message. When I criticise a "bling materialism"[8] prevalent in parts of the inner city, what I am really trying to communicate to young people is that it proves nothing. Respect must be earned, not bought over a counter. These messages are about culture as much as politics.

Few parents either want to or imagine that we can go back to a pre-consumerist age – they don't believe that shopping is the root of all evil or that wanting to buy things makes you a bad person. An afternoon at the shops can be quality time with your children. Pocket money is one way that we teach our offspring that sometimes you can't have everything you want immediately. During my childhood Wednesday nights would see bundles of newspapers swamp the living room as the local weekly free sheet, the Haringey Advertiser, arrived in bundles for delivery. Mum would join my sister and me, donning a fluorescent satchel and gloves to ward off dangerous dogs, as we stuffed letterboxes across Tottenham. The paper round was an exercise in self-reliance: the idea that if you want something you have to work for it. How children spend the money amassed in piggy banks and savings accounts can also hold important lessons, teaching them to make their own choices and think beyond instant gratification to what will really make them happy.

Parents want to introduce their children to a consumer society on their own terms, however. Many feel hopelessly outgunned as they set about this task. I grew up in a world of four television channels. Our parents knew what we were watching. They heard the music we were listening to. They knew which magazines we could get our hands on. They could set boundaries around the influences on us. Today satellite and cable television beams nearly 700 channels into front rooms, creating endless possibilities when a child presses the "on" button. Product placement infiltrates entertainment as well as advert breaks. Online companies target marketing at children with forensic accuracy. Parents find themselves competing for their children's attention with the might of multinational industries determined to claim their share of the £99 billion market for children's consumer goods.[9]

The overwhelming majority of parents feel that companies target their children too much.[10] Ninety-two per cent are concerned that kids share too much information online.[11] The least those parents can expect is that government is not complicit in a culture where advertisers hassle children, hoard personal information and flood public spaces with consumer messages. This is the cultural cocktail that helps produce such materialism and makes parents' lives impossible.

Facebook's website promises potential advertisers the opportunity to "reach your potential customers and grow your fan base with highly targeted Facebook ads".[12] It makes this possible by trawling for information on people's personal profile pages, including what people list as their interests, favourite music, TV shows, books and films. It keeps a record of which groups people join and even uses data on religious beliefs to help clients aim their adverts more effectively.

For adults, some of these tactics may seem underhand. For the estimated five million teenagers who are on Facebook in the UK,[13] they are unacceptable. Rather than recoil from this, Facebook actively advises its clients how to market to the "high school population". Having selected your "geographic network(s)", it explains, "you can then target your ad by age, selecting the age range '13-18' ".[14]

By the age of three, almost 70% of children have learned to recognise the McDonald's logo but less than half know their own surname.[15] By six, children are developing clear ideas about what is "cool".[16] By 10, the average child can recognise nearly 400 brand names.[17] By their teens, big business will have infiltrated their online social networks, using trails of data to predict and shape their habits. In economic terms the market works efficiently, neatly configuring itself around the desires of young consumers. The problem is that parents don't want their kids bombarded with adverts until they are old enough to put them in context. The question should not be whether the market is working as it "should", but what kind of society and culture this is producing.

Parents must be given the breathing space to shape their children's character and values without being constantly undermined by commercial influences. In the US, senators John Kerry and John McCain have put forward legislation for a digital bill of rights, giving people far more control over their personal data.[18] It is a bipartisan issue. In this country too, adults should have a much greater say over how companies store and use their personal information.

Children, meanwhile, need stronger protection. Greece doesn't permit stations to run commercials for toys between 7am and 10pm. Sweden has long prohibited all TV advertising aimed at children under the age of 12.[19] These ideas should be applied in Britain to prevent the manipulation of children by big corporations. In the United States, more than 1,500 towns and a number of states, including Vermont, Maine and Alaska, all prohibit the "visual pollution" of large billboards in public spaces.[20] In

Britain, local residents should decide whether huge posters pushing consumer messages add to the character of their neighbourhood or detract from it. The government cannot bring up people's children, but it can give parents a fighting chance to make a success of it themselves.

Filling the void

I will always remember appearing on Songs of Praise when it was held in Peterborough cathedral. I was given the opportunity to sing some of the greatest music ever produced, standing in surroundings I could once not have dreamed of, with my voice being broadcast across the UK. I could visualise my family setting the VCR at home in Tottenham after spending most of the week reminding colleagues and neighbours about my appearance. I was overwhelmed by pride. It was not for a prize, a record contract or a financial reward, but simply for what I was doing. I experienced, for perhaps the first time, the transcendence of applying myself completely to something. This was what I understood aspiration to mean: the urge to learn a craft, to do something brilliantly, to fulfil a talent through hard work.

Experiences like this are priceless for young people. This is why we should value the programmes for sport, art and culture in schools that teach children to express themselves in healthy, creative ways. The challenge is not simply to subsidise theatre trips or free entry to museums that give children access to culture that others have produced. It is about equipping young people to make their own mark. As culture minister in the last government, I was responsible for the Creative Partnerships programme, an initiative that brought artists from a range of disciplines into schools. The value of bringing children into contact with poets or drama groups was difficult to capture in the tables, targets and measurements that are the currency of decision-making in government. But these experiences, like mine in Peterborough cathedral, can transform lives, opening up passions that one never knew existed.

For young people of all backgrounds, to be exposed to true excellence like this is priceless. Already millions watch great films and post their responses on YouTube. People want not just to listen to music but to remix and play around with it. One artistic act inspires another. They are reaching towards something more meaningful than *buying* their identity. We should give more the chance to do the same. Given the choice, I would prioritise money for programmes like Creative Partnerships that encourage children to take part, not those that plonk them in an audience and expect the experience to make a difference.

Likewise, our civic institutions are vital in the battle against a shallow materialism. Robert Baden-Powell, the founder of the Scouts, described its mission as to foster a "spirit of self-negation, self-discipline, sense of humour, responsibility, helpfulness to others, loyalty and patriotism"[21] in young people. Modern Britain needs more institutions on the lines of the Scouts, the Girl Guides or the Boys' Brigade to ground youngsters in the habits of citizenship. No longer should we shy away from a universal civic service, with young people across the country visiting the elderly, helping out in schools, mentoring younger children and renovating public spaces.

After the riots, now is not the time for half-measures. The coalition government has committed itself to a civic service in name, but its plans come up woefully short of what is required. The programme is voluntary and is expected to last just seven weeks. Young people will have to pay to take part. The idea that a scheme like this will reach those involved in looting Tottenham Hale retail park is simply not credible. A British civic service must reach everyone. It should be compulsory and last around six months – long enough to make a real difference to young people's lives. Participants should be paid the minimum wage to ensure that this amounts to more than a glorified gap year scheme for the well-off.

The scheme would not be cheap, of course, but as the riots proved, there are great financial and social costs associated with a culture in which materialism becomes the dominant value.

The bill for simply cleaning up after the riots has run into the hundreds of millions.[22] This is before the cost is counted to the criminal justice system, as offenders have been arrested, tried and often incarcerated. As a nation, we should be seeking to rescue the idea of serving others rather than simply helping ourselves. A national civic service would help address the gaping social deficit revealed by the riots.

More than a shopping mall

The riots were not "caused" by consumerism, and this is no clarion for the dawn of a new puritanism. The looters made choices and must be held accountable for them. Countless others from similar backgrounds, living with the same social pressures, never even considered going out to steal. For many, consumption can be a positive thing that binds us together. Supermarkets on a Saturday morning are filled with people buying food for the week for their families. Every parent appreciates the joy of giving to their children on birthdays, or exchanging presents with friends at Christmas.

However, consumption should supplement our relationships, not become a substitute for them. For too long we have allowed the currency for affection to become pounds sterling. Parents frequently dread the run-up to birthdays and Christmas, worrying whether the overdraft can absorb another round of gifts. Too many of us have become caught up in a competition that has no winners – for status and respect based on the brands we wear. It has led to an overworked, overindebted and often unhappy society.

It is not the job of government to be the arbiter of people's everyday choices. Ministers have no place telling people how to spend their time or money. But the images of thieves trying on clothes while others piled loot into shopping trolleys must serve as a wake-up call. The very least that politics can do is to support those parents who want to teach their children that we are more than consumers – and that society is something bigger than a shopping mall.

CHAPTER 6

RIGHTS AND WRONGS

Common decency versus the letter of the law

In 2006 Tony Blair asked me to help Britain apologise for slavery. The nation was approaching a milestone. The following year was the bicentenary of the abolition of the transatlantic slave trade. Britain, of course, had led the fight to end slavery, but only after a century of buying and selling human beings. Two hundred years later, a prime minister had agreed it was time to say sorry.

My ancestors were among the 12m Africans forcibly transported to the plantations of the Caribbean. Three million travelled on British boats.[1] One in five didn't survive the journey, dying chained up on the vessel that they travelled on.[2] When I was asked to take the lead in the government's efforts that year it didn't take long for me to say yes. In the end the PM played it safe. The legal advice was that a full, formal apology might open Britain up to lawsuits demanding reparations. The US has a long history of such litigation and the prime minister was cautioned against any full admission of culpability. He expressed "deep sorrow" for the British government's complicity in the trade. "It is hard to believe that what would now be a crime against humanity was legal at the time," he reflected.[3]

I spent the year determined to tell the full story of abolition. History has rightly revered men like William Wilberforce, the social reformer who led the fight in parliament. But the slave trade was not simply abolished by a well-meaning group of parliamentarians. Former slaves like Olaudah Equiano wrote movingly above the evils of the trade, inspiring ordinary people to make their voices heard. Across Britain they did: in 1792 more than 500 petitions were presented to parliament, including one from every single English county. Three hundred thousand households refused to buy sugar produced through the slave trade.[4] People wrote letters and joined marches calling for abolition. The new rights and freedoms of enslaved people were not granted by accident – they were demanded by one of the most successful reform movements in history.

While the PM was deploring crimes against humanity, he was also preparing the ground to rewrite the Human Rights Act (HRA). His concern was not that people's rights were too weak, but that they were too strong.

Downing Street had described some recent court rulings as "barmy" and the PM was losing patience. In a letter leaked to the newspapers, he ordered the home secretary to lead a review of the HRA, making it one of the government's key priorities.

The news was reported breathlessly in the media. Human rights lawyers labelled the move "sinister" and warned against "the worst excesses of authoritarian government".[5] But unlike their forebears they were not swept along by a vibrant popular movement. Crowds did not take to the streets. There were not hundreds of petitions. A small group of lawyers found themselves defending something that has become increasingly unpopular.

More people agree than disagree that "the only people who benefit from human rights are those that don't deserve them".[6] The most common interpretation of the Human Rights Act is that it represents "political correctness".[7] Seventy-five per cent of Britons think that the act "is used too widely to create rights that it was never intended to protect", while just 12% feel it is used "about the right amount to protect rights which are necessary for the individual's protection".[8] Prime minsters who complain about human rights legislation rarely worry about the political backlash.

'Phoney human rights'

So it was with the riots. David Cameron stood on the steps of Downing Street, hot off the plane from Tuscany, to address the nation on the brink of the fourth night of lawlessness. His first statement would be his most important. He had to convince a fearful public that his return would signal the end of the worst of the troubles. On crime at least, this was by far the sternest test of his premiership to date and it was telling that he used human rights as his straw man.

"Picture by picture these criminals are being identified, arrested," he reported, promising sternly: "We will not let any phoney concerns about human rights get in the way of the publication of these pictures and arrest of these individuals."[9] In practice there was never much danger of this. The rights laid down in the HRA must each be weighed against the wider public interest, which in this case was overwhelming. Few legal experts suggested that the photos would not be published and it was no surprise when the police put them online a few weeks later. But that wasn't really the point.

Later that week, in a more reflective speech, the PM returned to his theme, arguing that in any discussion of the causes of the riots, "We inevitably come to the question of the Human Rights Act and the culture associated with it."[10]

Clearly the No 10 pollsters hadn't been abroad. This was a lament that I had heard time and again after the riots. In conversations in community centres, in minicabs and in cafés people blamed the riots on a "rights culture" in general and human rights in particular.

People who had seen the police stand off from rioters, content to contain disorder rather than put a stop to it, felt that human rights concerns had not protected residents but put them at risk. Some felt that a rights culture had created a sense of entitlement to everything, as exemplified by the looting. Others saw young men and women stick two fingers up at authority and blamed the movement to ban parents smacking their children on human rights grounds. As he laid into "phoney human rights claims", the prime minister was putting his finger on these concerns.

A week later the tone was different as the PM made another statement from the same lectern in Downing Street. His subject this time was the unfolding crisis in Libya. "I spoke to Chairman Jalil [of the National Transitional Council] last week," he told the cameras, "and will be speaking to him again, to agree with him the importance of respecting human rights."[11] One week before human rights were the problem; this week they were essential and had to be respected. The echoes of Cameron's predecessor were strong. Tony Blair passed the Human Rights Act but became increasingly frustrated with it. He was willing to apologise for crimes against humanity in Britain's past, but reticent about the role of human rights in its future. David Cameron has been happy to take the moral high ground in international affairs, demanding that human rights be respected abroad. Yet he and his ministers have been willing, even eager, to lash out at them at home.

The problem for those who believe in the value of human rights is that criticising them has become an open goal. Prime ministers who find themselves backed into a corner lash out at them, knowing that they are on safe ground with the public. For many people, human rights are part not of a historic process of emancipation, but of an agenda cooked up and enforced by a distant elite.

Elitism

At the heart of this unpopularity is the idea that moral questions about privacy, torture or taxation can be turned into legal, procedural concerns, to be dealt with by experts. The mistake is to imagine that each broad human right represents a "truth" that can somehow be discovered by lawyers and judges, rather than a starting point for a much wider debate reaching well beyond the courtroom.

For example, some interpret the right to life as an argument for a National Health Service that saves millions of lives. Others think it justifies a ban on abortion. Neither can realistically be described as a "truth" that anyone could prove in court.[12] Campaigners on either side must make their cases to the public, through evidence and ethical argument. The idea that there can be only one correct interpretation of these things – and that finding it should be left to the experts – is a view that, at its most extreme, sees democracy as a distraction, or even a barrier to doing what is objectively "right". The courts must keep society virtuous, whether we like it or not.

Some of the anxiety around human rights has been driven by media reporting that has been less than accurate, from wrongful accusations of a prisoner being given access to pornography on human rights grounds[13] to incorrect suggestions that human rights prevented parents from filming nativity plays in schools.[14] But neither an overexcitable media nor populist politicians can be blamed entirely for the deep unpopularity of human rights in modern Britain.

Public sentiment has been driven by a series of recent cases. People see attempts to force a smacking ban under the auspices of the right to freedom from torture,[15] and it does not feel open or democratic. They do not feel that a right inspired by the horrors of the gas chambers in Auschwitz should be updated to address questions about how they bring up their children. The same people see bankers challenge taxes on City bonuses citing the right to "peaceful enjoyment of possessions" and are understandably shocked.[16] They find the idea that such cases are even plausible offensive after a financial crisis that has cost so many their homes and their jobs.

The results of these cases matter and the Human Rights Act is normally balanced enough to produce a final judgment that most of us agree with. But what concerns people is the possibility that a broadly defined human right might be manipulated in the courts to undermine laws made by a democratically elected government.

Liberals may well want to ban smacking outright. Bankers may well want to avoid taxes. But no one voted for these policies. No elected politician put them in a manifesto. Instead they are the priorities of those who seek to get their way without bothering to persuade everyone else. It is a model of social change driven not by open argument, deliberation and persuasion but rather by the most skilful lawyers.

What those who refuse to engage with this public sentiment – or, worse, wear it as a badge of honour – forget is that rights are only sustainable when people feel ownership over them. They should enshrine notions of social solidarity and mutual respect, not replace them. In Britain historic battles have been fought and won – from free speech and trial by jury to the right to treatment on the NHS – but these rights are sustained only by those who believe in continually making the case for them through the democratic process. It is when public persuasion is replaced by legal wrangling that rights become vulnerable.

The riots revealed, once again, that many people feel embattled rather than protected by human rights. There is a feeling that commonly held values are being eroded and disregarded by an elite that believes it knows better. If we continue to set human rights up in opposition to democracy, they will always be vulnerable, always be unpopular, always be blamed by prime ministers who find themselves in a hole.

Claims, not truths

Questions about how forceful policing should be when order breaks down, or whether parents should be permitted to smack their children, are moral dilemmas before they are legal ones. They are questions of politics before law. The courts must implement laws when they are made – fairly and impartially – and inevitably this involves some degree of interpretation. The law inevitably evolves as individual cases set precedents. But all of this should be within a framework of legislation set by the elected representatives of the people, not judges who are answerable to no one.

To restore this sense of democratic accountability – and the belief of constituents like mine that their concerns will not simply be dismissed – governments must stop hiding behind the courts. Whatever the perceptions and the anger in the wake of the riots, the truth is that the courts have no power to demand that the law be rewritten on human rights grounds, let alone rewrite it themselves. They can declare that legislation is incompatible with human rights, but this is where their powers end. It is governments that have subjected themselves to the judges, choosing the easy path of grudging compliance rather than standing up for what they believe in.

After the riots, the prime minister declared himself willing to stand up to "phoney human rights claims" – but this was a departure for ministers who have often preferred to grandstand in criticism of the courts and then bow to them anyway. When the European Court of Human Rights produced a ruling on votes for prisoners, the prime minister claimed that the idea of allowing prisoners to vote made him feel physically ill. He explained his view that "when people commit a crime and go to prison, they should lose their rights, including the right to vote".[17] But rather than stick to this point of principle – right or wrong – ministers took to the airwaves to protest that Britain had "no choice but to comply with the law".[18] In truth they did have a choice: the HRA gives governments, not the courts, the final say.

Human rights should provoke democratic debate, not override it. They should be tools to make governments more accountable, not less. The courts should not be able to strike down legislation using human rights law – but they must be able to force governments to face up to issues, like votes for prisoners, that they would rather not discuss. Ordinary people should be able to petition the courts to force an issue on to the political agenda. When a court declares a law incompatible with human rights, that law should automatically be debated and voted on in parliament. Parliament would not be overruled, but it would be asked to discuss and vote on the issue again. In the unlikely event that the courts had declared the publication of rioters' photos incompatible with human rights, for example, the automatic response should have been for parliament to debate the law around privacy and, if necessary, amend it for future cases.

Similarly, in individual cases where companies breach human rights, the courts should trigger debates about whether regulations ought to be changed or left the same. At the moment no such debate takes place. When judges declare a piece of legislation incompatible with human rights law, the only consequence is that this ruling must be noted on the front page of the legislation itself. The idea that this has any real effect is farcical – it has zero impact on public consciousness and is barely reported in the media. A debate and a vote in parliament, with all the attention they create, would be a far bigger step towards reuniting democracy and human rights, helping the courts to become a voice for the ignored, not a forum for elites and special interests.

The public must be able to see this process in action to fully trust and understand it. Already the sentencing of rioters and looters has led to confusion and disillusionment. We rely on patchy reporting from journalists in court and briefings from the Ministry of Justice, with many people remaining both distant from and sceptical about the legal process. This is the environment in which human rights can become such an easy target for both the press and the political establishment.

Rather than expect people to take for granted that their concerns have been dealt with, we should televise court cases. We already allow the public to visit the courts, so there is no reason why adding cameras would represent a threat to justice. People should be able to switch on the TV set or their computer to watch the legal process in action. As a society we would become less reliant on either politicians or the print media to frame debate. Judgments would be far more likely to feature on the television news. This would tackle some of the myths that surround human rights and bring people closer to a system that often feels detached.

Televising the courts should go hand in hand with a final reform bringing a great deal more honesty to the role of judges. If we accept that human rights are not facts to be discovered by experts but moral claims to be debated, then those who pass judgment on human rights in court are unavoidably part of a political process. How they interpret the boundaries of privacy or the implications of the right to life matters. The problem is not just that the judiciary is so unrepresentative of wider society (one survey of top judges found that all were white, 98% were male, 84% went to Oxbridge and three-quarters had a "full house" – white, male, public school and Oxbridge).[19] What is just as troubling is that we have no idea what they think.

The US system is more honest. Senior judges go through confirmation hearings in which elected politicians ask them to set out some of their broad assumptions and prejudices. There is an explicit recognition that we all have inclinations and biases that influence the judgments we make. Making these public helps sift out those with extreme attitudes and implicitly encourages judges to guard against pushing their own views too hard. We should adopt the same practice for senior judges in Britain, with prospective high court judges going through confirmation hearings in parliament, which would themselves be televised. Only then will human rights be restored to their proper place in a democracy: as moral claims, debatable questions, not the latest set of preferences of an unaccountable judiciary.

Rights talk

The final part is the hardest. When people bemoan a "rights culture", they are talking about something more than the workings of the Human Rights Act. It is a sense that people are too willing to disregard the implications of their actions for others – that, to some degree, society struggles even to have a conversation about right and wrong, beyond whatever the law happens to say at the time. We cling to the idea that we are "within our rights" rather than considering what the right thing to do might be.

The riots demonstrated this once again. After two full nights of rioting, I called for the telecoms company Research In Motion (RIM) to suspend its Blackberry Messenger (BBM) service for just a few hours. BBM was being used by rioters to coordinate looting, allowing them to send encrypted messages to one another and outfox the police. I took the view that the company ought to recognise its responsibility to the rest of society and suspend its services at night, even if that meant upsetting some of its customers for a day or two. Some of the reactions to my suggestion were remarkable. My Twitter account suddenly came alive, as people felt compelled to get in touch telling me that I was a "disgrace". Most accused me of demanding state censorship. Some drew direct comparisons with Hosni Mubarak, the former president of Egypt, who had responded to a civil uprising against his regime by shutting down access to the internet and mobile phone networks.

Except I hadn't called on the government to do anything. I had simply appealed to the company to do the decent thing. I was asking not for state censorship, but for corporate responsibility. It was a question of ethics, not law. I was asking for RIM to think beyond the legal position and consider the shopkeepers and residents around the country who were terrified that their neighbourhood would be next. Of course suspending the network was not a long-term solution. But for a few hours, perhaps even a few days, it might have helped disrupt communication between the looters who were running rings around everyone.

For many this didn't simply didn't compute. The issue was straightforward: either I was calling for a change in the law and should therefore join the ranks of the dictators – or I wasn't and whatever RIM did was none of my business.

The company was within its rights to keep the network live and I had no right to tell them what to do.

This is how hollowed out our political debate has become. Of course RIM had the right to keep its networks alive. But having the right to do something does not make it the right thing to do. We should have learned the consequences of mistaking these two things by now. The financial crisis was caused by actions that were mostly legal, but still greedy and reckless. During the expenses crisis, many of the claims made by MPs that most infuriated people were not criminal – they were within the rules. In our everyday lives we each rely not just on freedom of speech but also on notions of politeness, civility and respect for others. Only in a dictatorship can the law police every aspect of morality. Yet too often, in an individualistic culture, we are content to reduce important moral debates to questions about what is legal rather than what is ethical.

Rights are one way that, as a society, we make unequivocal moral judgments. They have done incredible things for Britain. They have helped reduce racism, sexism and homophobia; they have improved working conditions for millions; they have improved the treatment of people by public authorities. But they can only take us so far. Laws can gesture towards the kind of society in which we want to live, but they absolutely cannot become the only arbiters of what is right and wrong.

The two revolutions that have shaped modern Britain – the economic liberalism of the 1980s and the cultural individualism that emerged from the 1960s – produce a shrill society unless they are ameliorated or moderated by something else. A focus on freedom, without any sense of duty or responsibility to others, is precisely what people are worried about today. It is this culture, at its most warped and extreme, that many feel lay behind the riots.

An honour

To supplement our individualistic rights culture, our society needs to reconnect with other important, informal regulators of behaviour. Notions of decency towards others. Pride. Shame. Admiration. Scorn. Different societies have always encouraged certain virtues, from the courage and prudence singled out by the ancient Greeks, to the mercy of the Romans and the thrift of the Victorians.[20] They understood, as we must, that people are social animals. We do things, in part, because of the effect they will have on our reputation. We give money to charity because we believe in good causes but also because we all enjoy public approval. We refrain from tempting acts of selfishness because we don't want others to think ill of us, because the disapproval makes us feel uncomfortable. These social emotions can reach the parts of society that laws cannot and often should not, encouraging everyday acts of self-restraint, self-censorship and self-regulation.

Such ideas need not be alien to politics. The idea of an "honour" has a long heritage in Britain – from monarchs recognising acts of service by granting their subjects money, land and titles to military honours awarded for distinguished service. Conversely, British society has always sought to harness notions of shame to prevent behaviour that is selfish, anti-social or illegal. The real punishment of an afternoon in the stocks was not the prospect of being targeted with rotten fruit; it was the humiliation of being punished in front of your peers.

In today's criminal justice system one of the attractive features of restorative justice, through which criminals are expected to repair some of the damage they have done, is that it connects with notions of pride and shame. It leaves offenders with no choice but to face up to the hurt and upset they have caused other human beings. It restores some sense that we are not just individuals who must obey the law, but part of a society that approves of some things and strongly disapproves of others.

Community punishments, when done properly, can connect with similar emotions. In the aftermath of the riots, looters should have been rebuilding Tottenham High Road on day release from prison. They should have been made to confront the damage they inflicted on the lives of their peers and expected to take some small steps, at least, to help put things right.

In other aspects of society where we see regulation as undesirable, we should explore how to promote ethical standards without coercion.

One of the lessons of the expenses scandal is the value of opening behaviour up to proper public scrutiny. The most effective and enduring move of all was to publish all future expenses online. The effect was not just more accountability but the introduction of an element of pride and shame as an informal regulatory force.

Modern politics must be much more inventive about harnessing these social norms to promote a sense of decency beyond simple compliance with the law. A freedom of information law for the private sector could shift the debate on from whether companies are within their rights to pay poverty wages or evade taxes, to questions about whether they are behaving properly and ethically. Newspapers, meanwhile, could be required to give the same prominence to the corrections that they make after printing untruths or mistakes as they did to the original stories. If an inaccurate story is front-page news, so too should the correction and apology be. We might end up with fewer misrepresentations of human rights laws, for a start.

A better conversation

The problem in Britain is not that we have too many rights. It is that we lean too heavily on them as a solution to every problem. Too often we reach for a legal fix to problems that are social and cultural. Our relationships with one another become adversarial and uncompromising. We lose a sense of decency. We justify being rude or inconsiderate because we have the right to free speech. We play music loud and late at night because we have a right to do so. We don't give up our seats on the bus because nothing in the law says we have to.

Our rights talk has led to a politics with too limited a vocabulary, too few ways of finding shared solutions to shared dilemmas.[21] In a more fragmented society, much less concerned with custom and heritage, the rights reflex is tempting. Rights provide rules that govern our interactions with people we don't know and very possibly don't trust. For those interested in a certain kind of freedom all this is deeply attractive. Rights help us take control of our own lives, allowing us to ignore social norms, conventions and expectations to pursue our own path.

The problem is that, important though these things are, they are not enough on their own. Over my lifetime many important freedoms have been won; we should not give them up lightly as a society. Nor can we forget, however, that a decent society is not just liberated by rights and freedoms but also nourished by a sense of respect and responsibility that holds us mutually accountable.

CHAPTER 7

BANGED UP

Punishment versus rehabilitation

At around 8.30pm on Saturday, 6 August 2011, Niche Mpala Mufwankolo went home. Tottenham Hotspur's pre-season friendly against Atlético Madrid had passed unremarkably. Some of the regulars had drifted into Niche's pub, the Pride of Tottenham, for a drink after the game, before slowly beginning to filter out at around 8pm. With the crowd gone, Niche decided he could allow himself some time off.

He had been home for less than a couple of hours when reports of the riots began to come through. What had started as a peaceful protest against the police had turned into something much more sinister, with cars and buses torched, civilians robbed and shops looted. Now the trouble appeared to be spreading. After a year and a half of work, the Pride of Tottenham had been open for only six months. Niche wasn't taking any chances and went back to check on his business.

He arrived to have his worst fears confirmed. Not only had the violence spread as far as White Hart Lane, but the pub's windows had been smashed and its doors kicked in. Inside a group of masked youths were ransacking the place, cramming bottles of alcohol into bags and trying to get into the till. Without hesitating, Niche confronted them, demanding that they get off his premises. Their response was not to run or to hide. It was to show him who was boss.

Knives were drawn. Niche began to fear not just for his property but for his life. Evading the mob, he fled upstairs, darting into the darkness of his office to hide. As he waited silently, he watched on the CCTV monitor as half the group continued ransacking his property while the others sought him out. All he could hear was the sound of doors being smashed in all around the house as the hunt continued.

Left with nowhere else to go, he scrambled out of the small window in his office and up onto the roof. There he lay still, watching through the skylight as his remaining stock was plundered. Only when the gang went could he leave his position too, climbing down the drainpipe outside the battered Pride of Tottenham.

Feltham

I have a responsibility to represent all my constituents, not just those I approve of. If caught, there is a good chance that those who terrorised Niche that night will end up in Feltham young offenders' institution, the high-security complex housed in the grounds of Feltham prison. My job will be to visit them there.

I have been going to Feltham ever since I became an MP in 2000. I go there mostly to listen. Talking with the inmates helps keep me alive to what is really happening on the streets of the inner city. In return, I do what I can to make sure the boys are treated as they should be while they serve time.

The first thing you notice when you walk into the room is their demeanour. They shuffle in without making eye contact. They look awkward as you reach across to shake their hands. They hesitate to introduce themselves, muttering their names. When they sit, they slump. As you talk, their concentration falters. They stare vacantly at you and around the room. There is none of the *faux*-confidence and swagger of the street.

Each time I visit, I go home wondering what the future holds for them. What sane employer would take them on, even if they make it out in one piece? What neighbour would welcome them? What woman would choose to start a family with them? They have so little of what it takes to succeed in modern Britain.

All service industry jobs require manners. Pret a Manger expects its employees to make eye contact with every customer, not to slouch, mumble and disengage. Call centres want employees with a phone manner, patience and application. So few of the Feltham inmates have any of this. Two-thirds of prisoners cannot add up to the level expected of an 11-year-old.[1] Half cannot read and write to that standard.[2] But this is just the tip of the iceberg: these boys lack the ability to relate to others at all.

Fathers are absent from many of these boys' lives and the mothers that trail in at visiting time are not coping. One in four prisoners in Britain spent some time in care as a child.[3] Half ran away from home.[4]

Ask the boys where they are from and you get a worrying answer. They don't reply with a road or a neighbourhood or a landmark. They give a postcode. Their territory. It is a reminder that though many come from fatherless homes, have been excluded from school and have little experience of legal employment, they do belong to something. They associate together in gang life. All this carries on inside, with gang members holed up in different wings of the prison to avoid constant outbreaks of violence.

Many of those I sit around the table with are in for offences every bit as shocking as the ordeal Niche Mpala Mufwankolo was put through. Once they have been convicted, most admit what they have done. There is no trace of sentimentality. As one 18-year-old boy – in for GBH – put it on my last visit, "Some of us committed crime because we had to, to get by. Some of us just chose to." After a pause, he added, "I chose it." For all their problems, they know they were faced with a moral choice – and that they flunked it.

Revolution

Two weeks after the riots the justice secretary was on the offensive. The disturbances, he argued, strengthened the case he had been making for a "rehabilitation revolution", encouraging prisoners like those at Feltham to go straight.

Armed with fresh data from the riots, he pointed out that 75% of over-18s arrested during the disturbances already had a criminal conviction.[5] Those who appeared before the courts had more than 16,000 prior offences between them.[6] One in three convicted rioters had already been to jail.[7] To the minister in charge this added substance to the argument that "simply locking people up for the sake of it is a waste of public funds"[8] and that "Too often prison has proved a costly and ineffectual approach that fails to turn criminals into law-abiding citizens."[9]

On his own terms, Ken Clarke's argument had been strengthened. The riots were yet another demonstration of how ineffectual our prison system is at turning lives around. Back at Feltham, almost eight out of 10 young offenders go on to reoffend within two years.[10] The boys count down the days until they will be released but the chances are that most will end up back inside. Nationally, more than half of all crime is committed by people who have been in prison before.[11]

Except not everyone sees the world like this. When I met Niche less than a week after the riots, I was struck immediately by his dignity. He is quietly spoken, tall, proud and impressive. As I introduced him to the latest group of dignitaries visiting the area, he crumbled as he retold his story, fighting off tears. A business that he had worked for two years to build had been shattered in a few moments by a selfish, nihilistic few.

For people like Niche, the first task of the criminal justice system is simple: to deliver justice. Government ministers may be able to construct a rational case for "intelligent sentencing", as they have taken to calling it. But rehabilitation is the last thing on the minds of those who have been robbed at knifepoint and had their livelihoods put at risk.

For them crime is more than a contravention of a set of rules laid down by the state. It is personal: the breakdown of the covenant we have with one another in a civilised society. The response to that cannot simply be to attempt to reform the individual, but to find a punishment that reflects the damage done to another human being.

This is about more than the length of sentences. In the wake of the riots judges sought to assuage an angry public with stiff penalties. Four years' imprisonment for posting messages on Facebook.[12] Six months for stealing a bottle of water.[13] But even these sentences do not reassure because the public do not trust that prison will be a proper punishment when offenders get there. When asked, a majority of people agree that "prison does not work" but the most popular solution is to make punishments harsher. Two out of three people say that prison doesn't work because sentences are too short and prison is too easy, whereas only half that number think prison doesn't focus enough on rehabilitation.[14] Eighty-one per cent of us say sentencing is "too lenient", while just 3% say it is "too harsh".[15] More people see rehabilitation as "a soft option that tries to make excuses for offenders rather than punishing them properly" than regard it as "a hard-headed, practical way of trying to reduce reoffending rates".[16]

These figures may be dispiriting for liberals interested in penal reform, but they cannot simply be wished away. Instead, the public must be involved in a mature, democratic conversation about crime, punishment and prevention. Reform of the penal system, like policing, must be done by public consent if people are not to feel angry and betrayed. Nor is this desire for punishment a moral failing on the part of those who have suffered. Retribution is a basic component of fairness. If you believe in a society of give and take, then just as reward should follow effort, the punishment should match the crime. The scales of justice are the very symbol of this – and we forget that at our peril.

Punishment versus rehab

Most fundamentally, the public's concerns are grounded in a truth no minister – in this government or the last – has liked to admit: there is a tension between punishment and rehabilitation.

I was responsible for prison learning as minister for skills in the last government. As part of my brief I took the usual pilgrimages to the Nordic countries to find out what we are doing wrong. The prisons there are a world away from ours.[17] The philosophy is that prison should mirror as closely as possible normal life. Unlike British prisons, where inmates spend much of their time in individual cells, prisoners in Finland, Sweden and Denmark often live together, cook together, do their washing together, learn together and spend leisure time together. In Denmark there are mixed-sex prisons with married couples living in dedicated wings. Children are even permitted to live with their parents up to the age of three. Unlike Britain, these countries have invested considerably in top-class facilities to teach inmates skills that will boost their chances of holding down a job. Relationships are built with employers, who sponsor programmes and take on inmates when they are released.

The purpose of all this is to teach inmates the habits of a civilised life, and in some ways it is very successful. Reoffending rates are far lower than ours. The problem is that it does not feel like much of a punishment. Good rehabilitation mimics real life but proper punishment does not. One of the central purposes of incarceration is to deny people privileges.

This tension – between rehabilitation and punishment – hangs over our criminal justice system. The public recognise it but those responsible for the prison system itself refuse to admit it. Caught between punishment and rehabilitation, we end up doing neither well. Instead the British penal system simply warehouses prisoners. Walk down most prison corridors and you hear nothing but silence. Prisoners sit alone in their cells for much of the day, doing nothing. The result is that many emerge at the end of their sentences neither as reformed characters, nor as chastened individuals fearful of ever having to go back.

Rather than pretend that this tension does not exist, we should accept it and restructure prison life accordingly. Punishment and rehabilitation should be separated so that we can do both properly. Sentences should contain two phases. First there should be punishment, in which privileges are withheld and prisoners face a gruelling regime. Only after this is completed should prisoners have the chance to earn privileges and graduate to rehabilitation. The two phases might take place in different places, with prisoners moved to rehabilitation units for the second stage of their sentences.

Though the final say must remain with judges, victims of crime should be given a voice in the punishment phase, with the option for prison sentences to include a restorative element, commensurate with public safety. Those who saw fit to vandalise the Pride of Tottenham should now be on day release repairing it. Ideally, they would be doing so in full view of the community, which would see justice being served. If we understand crime as the breakdown of social trust, then punishment should serve in part to repair it. Such schemes – often used as an alternative to prison rather than as part of a prison sentence – are often dismissed as gimmicks. But we forget that notions of pride and shame are powerful regulators of a decent society. In a civilised society, a fluorescent bib denoting punishment and reparation for a crime should serve that function.

Going to rehab

Only when the public requirement – and the moral justification – for punishment are recognised properly in our penal system will the government earn permission to do rehabilitation properly. Here too there are important lessons to learn from our recent past.

Inspired by my fact-finding trips to the Nordic countries, I led a big push in government on education training for former inmates. I began it full of hope. It felt like somewhere that government should be able to make a massive difference. As in most areas, there was no shortage of money. Spending on offender learning trebled during Labour's second and third terms in office.[18] And we had a captive audience, in a literal sense. Surely we could teach inmates the kind of skills that employers look for?

In September 2007 I took a trip to Bedford prison to check on the progress of one of our flagship schemes. The initiative we had launched would link offenders with employers, Nordic-style, who might take them on at the end of their sentences. Work experience would be built into inmates' daily routines, preparing them to start work when they had served their time. Prisoners would go out on day release, gaining practical experience on the job. Employers would have the chance to vet prospective employees.

During the visit I met Daniel, a 21-year-old convicted of a violent offence. Having shown remorse for what he had done and a willingness to reform, Daniel had been selected to take part in the programme. He had excelled in the structured environment offered by the programme, picking up an NVQ and securing a work placement. As I met him I felt we were really on to something. This wasn't learning detached from the real word – it had purpose and direction. Daniel was progressing well and the firm where he was doing work experience was making positive noises about taking him on. I left Bedford feeling cheered about what we were doing and asked my officials to keep me apprised of his progress.

Daniel served the rest of his sentence and went on to take up a role at the hi-tech engineering firm at which he had been working. He lasted just two months in the job. For years his life had been run for him. He had been told when to eat and what he was eating. He hadn't needed to get himself out of bed – he had no choice. He had rules of conduct to follow. Even the trips out on day release were structured by others. Faced with holding down a job in the real world, he couldn't cope. Despite my hope, his efforts and his new qualifications, the scheme had failed.

Daniel's situation was symptomatic of a wider problem. For too long the discussion about rehabilitation has treated criminality as an individual pathology. Just as patients must be cured of an illness, the assumption has been that individuals must be cured of the defects that led to criminality. It is telling that we still talk about rehabilitation rather than reintegration. It reflects the mindset of a peculiarly individualistic society that we look only at the individual, while ignoring the quality of their relationships with others. The model is a medical, not a social one.

To that end, billions of pounds have been ploughed into literacy classes and drug and alcohol programmes. Often the programmes have produced what looked like good results, with tens of thousands of inmates gaining qualifications and going clean. But what all this ignored was prisoners' relationships with others. It imagined people as units to be processed by a giant, impersonal machine, not as social animals who needed advice and constant support if they were to reform their lives on the outside. Many of them left prison with no money, no mentor, nowhere to live and no prospect of a job. In the absence of all this, they went back to the only people and the only life that they knew. This didn't show up in the "key performance indicators" measured by the Treasury, but it was a failure all the same.

Of course inmates must be taught to read, write and count, but many also need to be reconnected with family, work and community so that they can genuinely be part of society once again. Prisoners receiving visits from family members are almost 40% less likely to reoffend, for example.[19] But our prison system is not built for this. Instead we warehouse prisoners in huge complexes, often miles away from their families. Most prison buildings were designed not to teach people to live with and respect others, but to isolate prisoners for individual reflection. Despite some initiatives like the Bedford project, most learning is vocational only in name. Employers are rarely involved in sponsoring the schemes and, without the right incentives, are reluctant to take on former inmates when they can find perfectly good staff elsewhere with far less risk involved. Until we start attending to the social context to which prisoners return, not just the time they spend in prison, rehabilitation is always going to come up short.

Heron

Back in Feltham there is a glimpse of a better way. Heron wing, set up in 2009 and populated by just 30 boys aged between 15 and 17, is built around the idea that this final part of their incarceration will prepare them for life outside.[20]

To gain a place on the wing, inmates must have demonstrated a willingness to reform. In return, they spend the rest of their sentence under the specific objective of re-entering society. The wing has its own kitchen and laundry, where the boys are expected to prepare their own food and do their own washing. Days start at 7am, when they wake up to prepare breakfast. Workshops take place between 8am and 11.45am, where they are taught life skills like cooking, decorating and managing personal finances. Following lunch there are more lessons, in everything from literacy and numeracy to bricklaying and mechanics. At 5pm the evening meal is served, followed by a period of "association time", when inmates are allowed to socialise. After 90 minutes the boys return to their cells for a proper night's sleep.

Those who make it here are assigned "resettlement brokers" – experts who work with them not just while they are in prison, but also when they leave. The brokers' job is to provide the practical and emotional support necessary to help the boys reintegrate into the wider society. They assist with everything from repairing family relationships to sorting out benefit payments and ensuring the boys have a roof over their head when they leave.

The new model is producing results. Rather than leave inmates idle and isolated, Heron ensures they are work-ready and socialised. Rather than being left to sink or swim when they leave prison, the boys have continuity through trusting, respectful relationships. And rather than judging the scheme on the number of qualifications or drug treatments it churns out, the key test for the brokers is what matters to the rest of society: whether the boys reoffend or not. Slowly evidence is emerging that the model works: in its first year, Heron's reoffending rate was 14% – compared with 80% for Feltham as a whole.[21]

Show me the money

The biggest threat to the Heron model is money. Prison is expensive enough as it is – around £55,000 per inmate, every year, in places like Feltham where security must be very tight[22] – and initiatives like Heron are dearer still.

Reoffending by prisoners on short sentences alone costs the taxpayer up to £10bn per year;[23] reducing it by just a fraction would save hundreds of millions. But like all investments, the returns are uncertain. And like everything in politics, today's problems tend to trump those of tomorrow. The political imperative for bobbies on the beat always overrides the long-term promise of savings from helping prisoners go straight.

Away from London in Peterborough, they are testing a scheme as innovative and potentially as important as the methods used on Heron wing. Like everyone else, officials in Peterborough recognise the potential savings to the public purse from doing rehabilitation properly. But they are also pragmatists. Rather than wait for a government that defies the laws of political gravity, they are finding the money elsewhere. The premise is simple: if rehabilitation really does save money, then investors ought to be willing to fund it in return for a share of the savings.

The result of this idea is the country's first "social impact bonds". Four charities have been contracted to work with short-term prisoners to enhance their chances of reintegrating into society. They will receive education, life skills training and mentoring while inside. When they leave, the support will continue, with the organisations helping them to access benefits, find somewhere to live, repair personal relationships and get jobs.

Unlike Heron, the work is funded by a collection of voluntary sector and private investors, who together have put more than £5m into the project, which will work with 3,000 inmates leaving over the next six years.[24] The model is simple. The savings to the public purse from any reduction in reoffending will be split between the government and those who risked their money funding the schemes. Investors could earn a return of up to £8m if all goes well.

Critics argue that the temptation will be to focus on the low-hanging fruit – those offenders who appear the easiest to reform – so the challenge is to structure the scheme to avoid this. The benchmark being used in the first incarnation is the total number of crimes committed by the offenders taking part. The organisers say this provides incentive enough to work with those who are currently responsible for the greatest number of offences. They will be compared with a similar group of offenders from elsewhere in the country to judge the success, or otherwise, of the enterprise.

Together, these ideas could form the basis for reforming the prison system. Not a muddled system, caught between punishment and rehabilitation, but an honest one that performs these two functions properly and in sequence. Cash-strapped governments, meanwhile, would not be expected to put money into schemes for prisoners rather than police for communities.

Our prisons are one of the most unreformed public services. People lack faith in them, they are expensive and they largely fail even on their own terms. The riots are a wake-up call, not just for a rehabilitation revolution but for a proper public conversation about what prison is for and how we fund it. For Niche Mpala Mufwankolo and thousands like him, that conversation cannot start soon enough.

CHAPTER 8

BLACK AND WHITE

Why the riots could have been even worse

In politics, elections take you out of your comfort zone. The game-playing in parliament becomes a distant memory. The circular media interviews, with their shallow questions and non-answers, are left behind. It's just you and the voters.

Sometimes you are reminded why you entered public service in the first place. Encountering a constituent whom you have helped can give you a real lift as you head from door to door. You rediscover why you left behind your freedom, your privacy and your weekends. Sometimes, though, you have a conversation that stops you in your tracks. The day I met Scott during the 2010 campaign was one of those.

From the moment the election was called, ministers like me were dispatched throughout the country. We were reinforcements for seats that looked close but winnable for

Labour. Roughly twice a week I would make bleary-eyed daytrips to places like Newcastle, Nottingham, Derby, Leeds, Manchester, Thurrock and Slough, catching an early-morning train and returning in the dark for some late-night envelope-stuffing in north London.

I had made the usual early start, meeting up with Ross, our candidate in North West Leicestershire, and a team of 20 or so volunteers who had turned out to help. We had positioned ourselves outside the Belvoir shopping centre in Coalville. Ross and I stood there wearing the obligatory politician's smile and large rosette as we did our best to grab a couple of minutes of people's time as they emerged into the sunlight.

Talking to a group of politicos is usually a long way down people's to-do lists, so the balloons we were handing out were the main attraction. Parents out with their kids drifted reluctantly towards us. Scott was one of them, a lanky 22-year-old in tracksuit bottoms. He pushed his buggy with his two-year-old in it towards us, claiming a balloon and a reel of stickers and dutifully pausing for a chat. Our conversation was friendly, as we discussed the fortunes of our respective football teams. Spurs, my team, were on the up. Leicester City, his team, were hoping for promotion to the Premier League, but he didn't get to see them play so much these days.

It was clear that Scott wasn't into "politics" – not even vaguely. But now that he had stopped, you could see he was interested in discussing the things affecting him and his family. After all, here he had someone who was supposed to be doing something about them.

After a few minutes I sensed he was ready to get on with the rest of his day and decided to pop the question: who would he be voting for? In a matter-of-fact way Scott replied that he would be voting for the BNP. There was no hint of aggression, nor any sense of pride, embarrassment or shame – just a clear statement of where he would be marking the cross on his ballot paper.

Scott's response threw me completely. He didn't look like the National Front bullies that I had steered clear of as a youth. There were no Dr Martens boots. There was no scowl, no skinhead. And yet he would be voting for a party whose leader has described mixed-race children, such as my own, as "the most tragic victims of enforced multi-racism".[1]

I asked Scott why. His response was equally matter of fact. Since the age of 16 he had worked as a labourer in construction. Now he had a wife and two children but could not find work to support them. Eastern European builders were getting the jobs he felt should be his, with many working for less than the minimum wage, and he was fed up. He insisted he wasn't racist but he didn't think it was fair.

I did what I could to address his concerns, hurriedly rushing through the policies we had in place. Did he know there were opportunities for training, funded by the government, if he needed more skills? Did he know that immigration was now falling overall? Didn't migrants create jobs as well as take them? It was one of those occasions you dread as a politician. You can hear your own voice while you are talking and it sounds hollow. The solutions that look so comprehensive on a briefing paper suddenly feel so partial and imperfect when exposed to the reality of people's daily lives.

We ended the conversation on good terms as Scott thanked me for the balloon and shook my hand. As he and his son disappeared into the crowd, his words echoed in my head. "It's not fair." I went home feeling seriously down about Labour's election prospects and bleaker still about Britain.

Why did Scott and others like him feel so disenfranchised? It simply wasn't true that the mainstream parties had ignored immigration. The Conservatives had based a large part of their 2005 election campaign on the issue. I remember being confronted everywhere I went by posters declaring in scrawled handwriting, "It's not racist to put limits on immigration." In the 2010 campaign David Cameron had promised a cap on immigration, even if he couldn't say exactly what the number would be.

For Labour's part, there was no shortage of action. In every term in office we passed at least one immigration act. Tony Blair made countless efforts to reform the asylum system. Gordon Brown had gone even further with his infamous promise of "British jobs for British workers", much to my discomfort. But neither the reforms nor the crass rhetoric had cut through. Growing numbers of working people across the country felt not just culturally adrift from Labour but unable to put their faith in any mainstream political party. We had all failed. Scott's decision to vote for a racist party was not just a reflection on him or his circumstances; it was a horrifying indictment of British politics.

The general election proved a false dawn for the BNP. In North West Leicestershire, Labour lost badly but the BNP could only come fourth. [2] Around the country an organised cross-party effort drove them out. More than 4,000 people donated to the nationwide Hope Not Hate campaign. [3] Volunteers flooded BNP strongholds in places like Dagenham in London, where 6,000 people received knocks on the door reminding them to vote on polling day.[4] The campaign was gutsy and organised, preventing the BNP from gaining a foothold in national politics.[5]

What successful electioneering cannot do on its own, however, is address the fear and insecurity that groups like the BNP feed upon. The election results were a success, but they succeeded only in putting the lid back on the pressure cooker.

Riot squads

Eighteen months later the lid was off. While the police dithered in response to riots and looting, residents came together to form vigilante groups. In Enfield, north London, 500 people patrolled the town in three groups. As they marched around the town, they chanted, "England, England, England..."[6] The suspicion that the mob had been organised by the English Defence League, the thuggish successor to a waning British National Party, was confirmed by a second chant of "E... E... EDL", the mantra of the Defence League.[7]

The following night, the EDL helped coordinate the "defence" of Eltham in south-east London. Up to 50 members of the league claimed to be leading up to 400 other residents in protecting the town from looters.[8] "This is a white working-class area and we are here to protect our community," said one of those on the streets.[9] That evening a bus containing three innocent black youths was attacked. The explanation given: they "looked like looters".

As if to prove it could still capitalise on moments like this, the British National Party swung into action, printing leaflets decrying unrest caused by "black gangs".[10] The reality that less than half of those rioting were black[11] made no difference to the BNP: the front of the pamphlet showed a man being forced to strip by a black rioter. The back made promises that the BNP would "bring the army in (*our* war is at *home*)".[12]

I do not intend to inflate the successes of either the EDL or the BNP. We shouldn't be so lazy as to assume that every gathering of white men must necessarily constitute a race hate march. Nor can you blame people for wanting to defend their neighbourhoods. Those nights the police were stretched beyond measure and no doubt the majority who went patrolling in Enfield and Eltham had the right intentions. But neither can we simply dismiss this as a handful of extremists. Like it or not, the presence of the English Defence League those nights went unchallenged.

Beyond Enfield and Eltham, other groups were huddling together. Turkish shopkeepers in Hackney, east London, closed their shops for the night, lining Kingsland High Street with baseball bats as they sat in wait for rioters. Bangladeshi residents and shopkeepers chased off would-be looters in East Ham and Bethnal Green, east London. Several hundred Sikh men gathered to defend their temple in Southall, in the north of the city, brandishing hockey sticks and ceremonial swords that would have frightened off even the most reckless of thieves.

In some ways these were examples of real and admirable civic pride: a determination to stand up for the majority who wanted nothing more than to carry on with their lives. As one of the Sikh group told the television cameras, "We are not here just to defend our temple – we are here to defend the whole of Southall." [13] But for all this there was something worrying about the way people chose to come together.

For the most part, people sought refuge and expressed solidarity and defiance within an ethnic community. The enemy was from outside. When three Muslim men died outside the mosque they were protecting in Birmingham, rumours spread quickly that the car that killed them was being driven by a black man.[14] Dangerous talk of "revenge" began to circulate, with worrying echoes of the Lozells riots six years before.[15]

Only the courageous and dignified speech made by Tariq Jahan, whose son Haroon was one of the three men killed, was enough to calm the tension. "Today we stand here to plead with all the youth to remain calm, for our communities to stand united," he urged. "This is not a race issue. The family has received messages of sympathy and support from all parts of society."[16]

These were not race riots. But they could have been. There was more than one moment when a racial powder keg was close to exploding. We were lucky that looters and "patrol groups" never encountered one another in Eltham and Enfield. We are lucky that the rioters chose not to target the Turkish shops in Dalston. We were lucky that men like Tariq Jahan stood up to lead.

The riots did untold damage to people's livelihoods and sense of security, but we were close to something even more catastrophic. We were very close to adding a racial dimension, which could have done more damage to people's trust in one another than we can possibly conceive.

'The Feds'

I am, of course, the son of immigrants. My father arrived in Britain in October 1956 at the age of 24. He joined 12 other young men on an old Dakota DC–3 warplane from Guyana to Trinidad, before boarding the steamship SS Luciana. Six weeks later it docked at Genoa in Italy. From there he made his way by train and boat to rainy Southampton, and on to a cramped doss-house in Stoke Newington, north London. Mum arrived much later. Aged 32, she landed at Gatwick in December 1970 to a hostile winter and a routine strip search. Born in a small village on the banks of the Demerara river, she was a country girl at heart, swapping rural Guyana for a life in London that was way beyond her experience.

I saw through my own mother the contribution that newcomers can make to a nation and the pride that comes with British citizenship. One day, aged 10, walking back from school, after discussing the unfolding news of the war in the Falklands, I turned to Mum and said, "I suppose we're on the side of the Argentinians, because we're South American?" Her response was to slap me across the back of the head, snapping, "Don't you dare talk like that at school!" Like so many who made the long journey to the UK, she was fiercely patriotic about her new home.

I inherited a positive view of immigration, but not a naive one, growing up well aware that the enthusiasm that my parents' generation had for Britain was not always reciprocated. Before he left, my father would often talk of the tumultuous period that coincided with his arrival in Britain. While he settled into a small flat in Finsbury Park, there were race riots taking place across London in Notting Hill. New migrants from the Caribbean had moved into the area, living alongside the white working-class community. Tensions had risen as landlords refused to rent rooms to black families, eventually spilling over into violence, hundreds of arrests and terrible setbacks to race relations in Britain.

During my own youth I remember my mother's accent being mocked when she came to visit me at boarding school in Peterborough. It reinforced my self-consciousness at being something different from the others. I was the only black boy in a whiter-than-white world and had to get used to the racial insults some of the older kids would subject me to. As well as "golliwog", "coon" and "nigger", they introduced me to the South African slur "kaffir". Like many black kids in that era, the playground insults were something I learned to live with and shrug off as best I could.

My mother's response was to tell me I had to work harder. She had no time for self-pity or for blaming people for their ignorance. In her eyes, the best way to silence the bigots was to be one step ahead, top of the class, beyond the limitations anyone tried to set for me. "You have to be twice as good as the others," she would say. "You have to work twice as hard. No one is going to hand this to you." Mostly her words would inspire me: I would redouble my efforts, determined to succeed despite the expectations of others. Occasionally, though, I would blow up, taking my frustrations out on her. "Why should it be any different for me?" I would demand.

The race riots of the 1980s grew out of this atmosphere. My parents' contemporaries had been dutiful and respectful of authority, even when it was less than respectful of them. The generation born in Britain but still not accepted by it was starkly different. There was a sense of being deprived in the active sense of the word – by someone else.

We had no recourse to talking of "back home" or that sense of determination that comes with the tough decision to move halfway across the world. We floated instead in a rootless limbo, strangers to the lands we were too often told to "go home" to, and feeling singled out by the country we had spent our whole lives in. This sense of alienation had some powerful symbols. My generation watched knowingly as John Barnes had bananas thrown at him while he wore a Liverpool FC shirt. He was an England international at the time.

This potent mix of cultural opprobrium, economic disenfranchisement and conflict with authority was and is refracted by American popular culture. At one of end of the spectrum films like Do the Right Thing[17] and Crash[18] have helped tease out the problems and nuances of racism, dramatising them and bringing them to a wider audience. Cultural dialogue through film and music has nourished reflections about race and disadvantage. But at the other end of the spectrum, parts of popular culture have served to perpetuate and entrench the problems, rather than ameliorate them.

Aside from the "get rich or die trying" culture propagated by mainstream rap acts, there exists a more sinister strand of rap music that reproduces a narrative of dispossession and nihilism. That some of these rappers are themselves former criminals can send out confusing messages to young black children. Many black girls and boys continue to face a culture of low expectations, not to mention the economic hardship they share with working-class kids from all backgrounds. But their chances of reaching their potential are diminished further by the idea, promoted daily on so-called "urban music" channels, that the system is rigged against them. No one wins if black children grow up believing that respect can be won only through fear, or that material wealth is reachable only through hustling and criminality.

It is a debilitating idea – one painfully in evidence in 2011. As shop windows were smashed in Britain's cities, social networks came alive with calls to strike back against the "feds". Teenagers lifting mobile phones and pairs of trainers from shop windows adopted the posture of American gangsters. Petty criminals deluded themselves that they were engaged in acts of resistance against "the system". Meanwhile, in the absence of the police themselves, vigilante groups mobilised to strike back. It was a chastening reminder of the chasm that can open up when an immigrant community and its neighbours find themselves living not in harmony but in conflict with one another.

Seats on the bus

"When a bus has only a few empty seats, the crowd trying to get on will push and shove; if there are many empty seats, the crowd will be courteous and considerate." So wrote Saul Alinsky, the American godfather of community organising, 40 years ago.[19] The pushing and shoving that Alinsky observed in bus queues are magnified 10 times over when people feel they are competing for a decent job or somewhere to live. This helped feed the racial tensions in Notting Hill more than 50 years ago and it goes to the heart of the immigration debate today. The chronic lack of good jobs and decent housing in Britain has turned the immigration debate toxic.

As I arrive at Westminster every weekday morning I usually pass Gladys, Dorothy and occasionally William working the early shift. All three navigate the corridors of power with Hoover, duster or bleach spray in hand. They are the House of Commons cleaners, who empty dustbins, clear away mouldy coffee cups and clean toilet rims as MPs and their staff stride into work.

Surviving on £7.85 an hour, they speak with conviction about life in London. Between them they waited 17 years for the papers that certify their right to remain in Britain rather than return to west Africa. Undeterred, they have been busy making a home and a life here. William, the most recent arrival, has just passed his citizenship test. Dorothy's daughter has just started reading business at university. Gladys is completing her level three exam in nursing.

By chance, two of the three are constituents of mine, living on housing estates in Tottenham. Their neighbours include members of the Windrush generation who came to Britain in postwar years, Eastern Europeans who came here as the EU expanded, and those who went to the local schools, grew up in the area and have seen their neighbourhoods change over the years.

They live in a community that has had the highest unemployment rate in London, with 16,000 people on the waiting list for council houses. Many of those who do work must find ways to live on low pay. Many of those who escape temporary accommodation end up living in conditions unfit for a family. These are neighbours who share the same problems. They have the same struggles to get by each month and the same hopes that one day they will have a house that they can call home.

The tragedy is that the common experience of hard work and low pay, of cramped houses and overburdened services, is a source of division, not solidarity. The scramble for resources – homes, jobs and school places – drives a wedge between those who have the least. People who contribute through hard work see a system indifferent to their needs. People who should be friends and neighbours become rivals.

For too long the culture in Whitehall has been to dismiss this. The government machine prefers to trust its own evidence base ahead of others' lived experience. If the data showed that migrants are net contributors to the UK economy – which I have no doubt they are – then the civil service has tended to see people's worries as irrational or ill-informed. In fact, the tension is not between truth and myth but between the general and the particular.

The winners of immigration have been those in the middle classes comfortable with the way Britain has changed, and employers who have benefitted from waves of cheap labour. The losers have been irregular migrants exploited in the black market, and working people who found their wages undercut and local services stretched to breaking point. The conflicting experiences of these groups are fundamental to the debate about immigration: the issue is not just how high or low immigration levels are, but who benefits and who feels they are losing out.

Without proper recognition of this, it is little wonder that immigration has soared as a public concern. In 2007 it reached a 30-year high, with almost half the public counting immigration among their top four concerns.[20] The figure was 3% in 1997.[21] Until the financial crisis at least, people rated immigration as a bigger worry than the state of the economy or the quality of Britain's schools and hospitals. It is the sense that they are being not just ignored but patronised and humiliated that drives angry men and women towards groups like the BNP and the EDL.

Dancers and pipe fitters

As a country we have yet to find a way to address these concerns. The new government talks tough on numbers, but fails to address the underlying dynamic of who benefits and who loses out from immigration. The government that I was part of made its own mistakes, believing that a points based immigration system (PBS), modelled on Australia's approach, would be the answer.[22] It wasn't and the system remains in place today.

Introduced in 2008, the purpose of the PBS was to manage immigration from outside the EU. Britain would grant visas to the highly skilled migrants who scored well on the points system, but not to those coming for jobs someone else could be doing. It was one of the policies I reeled off in my exchange with Scott, standing outside the shopping centre in Coalville.

To make the system work, a group of civil servants, business representatives and trade unionists would sit down every few months, consult a series of graphs and engage in crystal-ball gazing about exactly which skills the economy needed. The Home Office would then establish a series of criteria so that the government could scrutinise individual applications, determining who would be awarded visas and who would not.

When the system was introduced in 2008 the Home Office decided that Britain needed more quantity surveyors, dancers and choreographers, ship and hovercraft officers, pipe fitters and line repairers.[23] How anyone can ever work this out is beyond me. In modern economies jobs come and go. Sectors expand and contract very quickly. People retrain. One day we have a national shortage of plumbers, the next day streams of people are leaving jobs in the City of London to earn qualifications in plumbing. The system we had in place was trying to manage the unmanageable, predict the unpredictable.

Worst of all, it asked little of employers in return. Government bent over backwards to please the business lobby, helping fill those "skills gaps" that industry complained about. But rarely were employers challenged to train some of their own staff instead. Nor were they asked to contribute enough towards building the houses or paying for the extra school places that would be required. The idea was that the points based system would benefit Britain. In fact, as with the bank bailout, it was corporations that benefitted while the taxpayer picked up the tab.

I have a simpler suggestion. Rather than pretend that civil servants know how many more computer programmers or graphic designers the economy needs, the government should simply set a price for working visas for migrants from outside the EU. Some employers would decide to go ahead and pay the fee, creating revenue to build new homes and fund local public services.

Other employers would think twice, investing the money in their own workforces instead. If demand for visas surged, then the government could simply raise the price, creating a greater incentive for employers to look for solutions within their own workforces. Either way everyone would benefit. Businesses would still be able to hire the migrants that they really needed, but they would make a contribution to the rest of society in doing so. The money raised from a new visa scheme, requiring employers to give as well as take, would be distributed to the areas most touched by immigration, to relieve some of the pressures placed on schools, housing, GP surgeries and other local services.

A scheme like this, which distributes the costs and benefits of immigration more evenly, could help remove some of the venom from the immigration debate. People like Scott in Coalville might have more chance finding that job. Potential BNP voters in Dagenham might have more chance of owning their home, or finding the council house that they often feel they are being denied. Migrants like

Gladys and Dorothy would not be set against their own neighbours in the competition for resources.

Waiting in line

Creating more seats on the bus is one thing, but the rules in the queue still matter. Towards the end of Labour's time in office we spent a lot of time talking about fairness without ever making clear what we meant by the word. Where immigration was concerned, this only served to mask some important questions. When people complained that immigrants were jumping to the head of the queue for social housing, Britain's elite immediately dismissed their concerns. A study commissioned by the Commission for Equality and Human Rights seemingly vindicated the liberal view, finding that, "Overall, policies represented an attempt to prioritise the most needy at a time of severe shortage in the supply of social housing. In this respect, the allocation policies were fair."[24]

In one understanding of fairness – that all benefits and services should prioritise those in greatest need – this was correct. The problem was that this wasn't the way many people already on council housing waiting lists looked at it. To them the idea of being in a queue or on a waiting list meant something. Seeing others enter the queue ahead of them didn't seem fair. Not only had they waited their turn; they had also paid into the welfare state over the years.

These concerns are easily racialised. Groups like the EDL quickly turn them into issues of skin colour, religion and ethnicity when they can. This is what lies behind the chants of "England, England, England" in Enfield. But I have heard the very same complaints from people who arrived in Britain in the 1960s, 70s and 80s from former Commonwealth countries. Like my parents, many found themselves doing low-paid jobs and living in cramped conditions. With that strong sense that they have paid into the system, they feel aggrieved when they are told that their children have dropped down the waiting list because others are in greater need.

The views of these families, who come from all over the world, are not grounded in racism. They are communitarian. They are concerned not just with questions of need, but also with who has already paid into the welfare state and waited in line. For them membership of a community – and the entitlements that come with it – should be earned. This has nothing to do with people's race, heritage or religion. Rather it is based on an idea of reciprocity: give and take.

The problem that we experienced in government was between different notions of fairness. Most leading New Labour figures had grown up with a liberal view of fairness, centred on serving those most in need. Many of those actually waiting for council homes, by contrast, had an alternative view, namely that people's contributions had to count for something, as well as their circumstances. They did not want to make others homeless, but did want their contributions over the years to count for something.

Late in the day we began to acknowledge this tension. The eventual request to local authorities that their decisions take account of time spent on waiting lists was recognition of it. So too was the shift towards a system of "earned citizenship" through which migrants would learn British history and the English language and pay taxes before being granted British citizenship. With more courage we might have applied the same principles to the entrenched and divisive problem of illegal migration.

If the irregular migrants who already live here paid taxes, we would be £1bn better off.[25] Instead, their presence divides communities and stokes tensions about legal migration. With a set of strict conditions, I would support a one-off earned amnesty for migrants. It would not be a free pass. People would have to earn the right to stay, paying taxes for a period before becoming entitled to benefits or taking their place at the back of the queue for housing places. They would be required to speak English within a set period and would have to have a clean criminal record. But, vitally, they would be able to contribute to the areas they live in.

We cannot remain detached from the idea that contributing to a community should count for something: it is central to the worldview of those in places like Stoke and Dagenham and Enfield who believe their prospects and way of life are under attack.

Culture wars

This schism between liberal and communitarian worldviews also lies behind the debate about social integration. The Southall Sikhs may have been defending the whole of their neighbourhood but almost half the population of Southall itself is of Indian origin, and the borough includes the largest Sikh community in London.[26]

Faced with these debates about integration, liberals tend to emphasise freedom for people to live their own lives, while communitarians are more concerned with the social glue that binds us together. Liberals emphasise the right of newcomers to speak in a language of their choosing and to dress, associate and worship as they wish. Communitarians rarely want to challenge these rights but they do have other concerns. If newcomers are joining a community rather than just a job market, that raises the question of how to retain social trust and shared reference points amid increasing diversity.

I do not underestimate the value of the liberal position. It was the absence of proper rights against discrimination that helped sow the seeds of anger in the inner city in the 1980s. Its consequences were deeply divisive. But for too long Britain has paid too little attention to the need to reinforce shared values, norms and experiences too. What we need are new ways to build trust and common ground out of Britain's diversity.

This demands an encounter culture in which it becomes commonplace and rewarding to interact with people from other backgrounds, races and religions. This is what builds our trust in one another. It is the people who live in the most ethnically diverse areas who feel most positive towards ethnic minorities.[27] It is unfamiliarity, not incompatibility, that is the problem.

Requiring that people learn English as a condition of British citizenship is one part of this, but it is not enough on its own. Britain has to learn from the Caribbean experience and do the hard work to prevent new immigrant groups feeling marginalised. In particular, we have to be alive to groups who arrive in Britain from failed states. Many have little in the way of formal education or employment. Their children may not speak English. These groups cannot simply be left to sink or swim. Schools, local authorities, job centres, colleges and voluntary groups have to come together to provide the necessary packages of support to help them make a go of life in Britain. Fail to do this and we are storing up problems with another generation of disaffected second-generation immigrants.

In a more fractured society we also need new institutions to bring people together to build trust and respect. A national civic service, as discussed earlier, would be a huge step towards encouraging a whole generation of young people to start to think beyond their own postcodes.

Nor should we be embarrassed about making clear statements of national unity. I have never understood why we have not adopted the American convention of describing people's ethnic identity in dual terms. When someone is described as "African-American" in the States, there is a tacit recognition both of their heritage and of their full membership of the nation that they live in. Their heritage is African, their citizenship American. E Pluribus Unum. In Britain we should adopt the same idea, injecting into our culture and national discourse the sense that our citizenship is an important expression of what we all share.

These changes would symbolise a more self-confident national culture, characterised not by paranoia about "cricket tests" or defensive retreats into ethnic identities. Instead it would reflect the idea that new arrivals can and should add new layers to national culture, rather than be seen to be pulling it apart.

CHAPTER 9

BANKS AND BUREAUCRATS

Giving power back to people

The Union Point building rose over Tottenham High Road in 1930. Originally a London Cooperative Society department store, the impressive structure became a local landmark. When the department store closed, the bottom floor remained a shop but the rest was converted into flats.

I became fond of the building when I was growing up and it was a privilege to reopen it in 2003 as the River Heights Apartments. It represented a new dawn for Tottenham. The 26 homes were both affordable and decent – high-quality one- and two-bedroom flats, ideal for young professionals. The development above the Carpetright store offered residents shared ownership, meaning they could own half of their home and pay a small rent on the rest. In a local authority where 16,000 are waiting to be housed[1] and 10,000 council homes still have the original kitchens and bathrooms from the 1960s[2], the new flats offered a glimpse of a future of quality homes for all. They attracted a mixed community ranging from supermarket managers to lecturers, taxi drivers to graphic designers, hospital cleaners to bus drivers and the retired. This was Tottenham at its best.

The residents weren't too worried when trouble broke out near the police station on 6 August. That was a kilometre away, at the other end of the High Road.

From their third-floor balcony, Stuart and Lynn Radose could see a fair distance down the street. Even when smoke began to rise from the burning squad cars and double-decker bus, they saw no reason to be overly concerned about their own safety. Slowly, but surely, however, the disturbances crept up the High Road. They watched people smash windows, loot shops, set fire to buildings. What they did not see was a single police officer.

Alarmed, they rang the local police, only to be told that while they knew what was going on, they couldn't do anything about it. It was soon apparent that the riot would reach the Union Point building after all. Within an hour, looters had entered Carpetright, beneath the Radoses' home, and begun ransacking it. Stuart made a second call to the emergency services. He got the same answer: "We know what's going on, but we can't help."

By now the rioters had set the building alight. Others fuelled the flames with tyres they had stolen from a nearby garage. The 26 families in the River Heights development had no choice but to flee. Resident Omar Malik called the fire brigade three times. No one came. By that stage the disorder was so widespread that fire-fighters were working behind police cordons to protect themselves from being pelted with bottles and bricks while they tried to put out flames.

It was left up to the neighbours to help each other get out. Omar fled with his wife and his five-year-old son as the flames engulfed the building. The first fire crews arrived at around five in the morning, six hours after the first calls for help had been made. By now the building was little more than a shell and no one knew if all the inhabitants had made it out alive. Twenty-four hours later, the building collapsed. A week later samples of rubble were still being taken to check that no rioters had themselves died in the fire.

Throughout its history, the Union Point building stood for a better future, first as a cooperative that distributed profits among its employees, then as a housing scheme that offered affordable and decent homes for people of all back-grounds. In its last hours it will be remembered as a symbol of vulnerability. We never expect to have to call the emer-gency services, but when we do, we assume they will respond. The 26 families had worked hard and paid their fair share – they had kept their end of the bargain. That night they felt utterly abandoned by those charged with protecting them.

Answerable to whom?

Four weeks after the riots I sat in a crowded room as River Heights' former residents met the police. After initial statements from a senior officer, the residents were given a chance to tell their stories. Most wanted to know why the initial unrest had not been stamped out sooner – how some small-scale skirmishes with the police had descended into anarchy. Others had another concern: when they had run down the high street to tell the police in person what was happening at River Heights, they had simply been told to move along. Many talked of officers sitting in lines of police vans, more concerned with containing the violence than with stamping it out.

Earlier that year, many had watched the heavy-handed policing of comparatively mild disorder in Parliament Square. They felt that in Tottenham things were different. There was no urgency at the top. Senior officers may have been sitting round the table with them that afternoon, but in no sense did they feel answerable to those they were supposed to protect.

I have since seen some of the police footage of the violence that night. Watching it, it is impossible not to admire the bravery of many of the individual officers involved. At the back of their minds will have been the knowledge that the last riots in Tottenham saw the brutal murder of PC Keith Blakelock. Eight officers were hospitalised that night in 2011.

Many of the River Heights residents understood the sacrifices that had been made. But they also believed strongly, as do I, that there were failures of police leadership. A lack of urgency allowed a bad situation to get worse. What the riots illustrated is that there can only be trust when there is accountability. Without this, people will always wonder if their safety really comes first.

Accountability

The coalition government's response to this problem is to create a system of elected police commissioners. But the answer is not another cadre of politicians, who will each be paid more than £120,000 a year[3]; it is better use of what we already have. Police authorities should be merged with local authorities, with council leaders selecting police chiefs.

Police chiefs would act like chief executives – free to make their own independent judgments on nights like 6 August, but much more accountable for the success or failure of those calls. This would create a direct line of accountability between local people and their police officers, without either costing a great deal or running the risk of extremists being elected as "sheriffs" on small turnouts.

In today's less deferential society, asking people simply to trust the experts no longer washes. Patients no longer arrive at the doctor's expecting to sit quietly; we walk through the door with printouts from the internet, self-diagnoses and lists of questions. Mothers and fathers no longer go to parents' evenings expecting just to listen; we turn up with our own feedback for the professionals who teach our children. Sons and daughters are no longer just grateful that a care home has found the space for parents; we are increasingly demanding about the way our loved ones are looked after. We increasingly expect teachers, doctors and carers to be accountable directly to us, rather than to targets and instructions sent down from Whitehall. The lesson of the riots is that the police cannot be immune to these changes – instead they should embrace them as a foundation for rebuilding trust.

The same applies to the judicial system. When someone reports a crime, they should be able to track its progress through the courts, just as they might track a parcel ordered online. As I argued in the chapter 'Rights and Wrongs', the courts themselves should be televised, so that we can see justice being done. And, wherever possible, victims should have a voice. The goal should be to have a restorative element in the punishment of all non-dangerous offenders, agreed in consultation with victims themselves.

Most of all, the demand for complete transparency applies to the Independent Police Complaints Commission, which must work much harder to earn people's trust. The establishment of an independent body to hold the police to account was a step in the right direction. But there is profound scepticism about an organisation that has investigated 460 deaths during or following police contact – including 21 fatal shootings – without producing a single conviction.[4]

The only way to overcome this scepticism is for the IPCC to become the most open organisation in the country. It must learn to be much more responsive, asserting its independence and communicating with local people from the word go when an investigation is launched. On the evening of Mark Duggan's death the IPCC should not have been content with a press release and holding pattern. Spokesmen should have been appearing on the TV and radio, from the 10 O'Clock News to Choice FM. There should have been immediate contact with Mark Duggan's family, alongside the offer of legal advice.

In the short term, the IPCC must assert its independence as it investigates Mark Duggan's death. Beyond that, it must find ways to increase the public's trust in it. Next time a chief executive is hired, the interview panel should include representatives from both the police and families who have dealt with the IPCC in the past.

Together, these reforms would go with the grain of a country much less willing to accept that those in authority always know best. Some wish to turn back the clock, restore the deference that we once had for the experts who make difficult decisions on our behalf, but the change is irreversible. People must feel that the services for which they pay are answerable not to distant rules and regulations, but directly to them.

Banks

With their homes burned to their ground, many of the former residents of River Heights were fed by stretched local services and charitable donations. One such resident was Mei. She had lived at River Heights for almost two years and works as an access consultant. "People didn't want to sit about; they wanted to get a new place to live, settle down and move on with their lives," she said. For this they couldn't rely on the philanthropy of others – they were at the mercy of their insurers.

Things did not get off to a great start. Zurich, the company that insured the River Heights building, was obliged to find them housing. A week after the riots, with all residents either in hotel accommodation or staying with friends or family, Zurich arranged to meet with the residents and to discuss the policy. In answers to their questions, the 26 families understood that they would only be expected to pay the rental element. The loss adjustor was adamant that the whole experience would be cost neutral for them. Full owners like Mei acted in the belief that they would pay nothing at all. With matters seemingly sorted, the residents drew up budgets, found suitable properties and moved into new homes in early September.

Yet by the end of September, everything seemed to change. Zurich were demanding the payment of service charges and management fees. Zurich maintain that they have not changed their position – despite what the residents say – and that the payments required are standard practice, but this seems to miss the point. The residents believed from the offset that the entire exercise would be cost neutral for them and that they would be in the same position financially as they were before the riots. That, after all, is the point of insurance.

But this couldn't be further from the truth. Residents like Mei had their budgets cut by £100 a month, others by even more. Residents feel they made their financial plans on information that at best was obscure and at worst, changed. With their new tenancy agreements already signed for a minimum of 12 months, there was no chance of moving again to somewhere more affordable, and the residents have been forced to absorb the extra costs.

Worse was to follow. River Heights' former residents were informed by their banks that they would still be expected to pay mortgages for homes that no longer existed. Mei, like others, was refused a payment holiday. There would be no waiting for the houses to be rebuilt, no chance for people to get back on their feet. As far as the banks were concerned, they were owed money and the fire was not their problem. The residents were left with the prospect of having to pay both the mortgage on the homes they had lost and all the costs associated with the new flats they had moved into. For many who had worked hard in order to buy into an affordable housing development, bankruptcy beckoned.

Only after heavy lobbying, from both me and the residents, did the banks budge. The payment holiday that they offered was for just three months, while the rebuilding of River Heights is estimated to take two years.

Even this concession came at a cost, however. "They refused to suspend the interest that was accruing on the mortgages," Mei explains. "So even if we took up their offer, we'd end up paying more each month after the holiday ended." Mortgage repayments would be higher for the

River Heights residents than before their homes burned to the ground. "They were not supportive or understanding of the situation we were in. We were made to feel completely powerless," Mei concludes.

This would be a bitter pill to swallow at any time. But the 26 River Heights families each contributed to the bailout of the banks in 2008 and 2009. The average cost per family in Britain is thought to be in the region of £40,000, with the total cost rising above £850bn[5]. When it came to the families' turn to be bailed out, the banks wouldn't listen.

Because the banks were too big to fail they were able to privatise their profits but socialise their losses. The River Heights residents, entirely blameless for their own situation, were not powerful enough to stand up to the same institutions. Had they been multi-millionaires, the banks would no doubt have offered more favourable terms, rather than risk losing valuable customers. But the cost–benefit exercise produced a different result for the River Heights residents.

All this boils down to a single word: power. The banks had the power to drain money from the Treasury coffers; the families were powerless to stand up for their interests. For too long the notion of empowerment has been shrunk to a limited discussion about public services. No one underestimates the importance of choosing the right school for your child, or selecting the GP's surgery that is most convenient, but the reality is that we live most of our lives in the private sector. The tale of River Heights symbolises a wider story in Tottenham and in Britain: people feel disempowered not just when they are bossed around by "big government" but also when they are bullied and cast aside by corporate giants.

Returns on capital

The behaviour of the banks in the wake of the riots reflects something fundamental about capitalism. It is built on a very straightforward idea: maximising returns on investment. No room for sentimentality.[6]

This is the source of the many great strengths of a market economy. The pursuit of higher returns creates a restless energy that drives innovation. Companies continually experiment with new products to trade, new markets to sell in and new methods to drive down costs. For the most part we benefit. All this produces great products we enjoy and the jobs we depend upon. But the lesson of the River Height families is that the drive to maximise profits can be destructive as well as creative. When we do not have sufficient power to stand up for our interests, the companies that we hope will serve us can end up exploiting us.

This is hardly a lesson that needed learning in Tottenham, where local people have spent the past year fighting to keep their football club in its historic home. Tottenham Hotspur was started by a small group of men from the All Hallows church in 1882. The founders imagined their football club as a source of local pride and community spirit. They hoped football would help cultivate qualities of loyalty, application, teamwork and honest competition.

One hundred years later Spurs became the first British club to float on the Stock Exchange.[7] Today the club is owned by a tax exile who lives in the Bahamas. Each week fans still arrive to cheer on their team. Stretched families shell out for tickets, replica kits and memorabilia. Grown men and women shed tears of joy and sadness as the team's fortunes wax and wane. But in the modern game, clubs show none of the same loyalty to the fans who cheer them on, or to the areas they grow out of. If the Norwegian owners of Wimbledon FC think they can make more money in Milton Keynes, then that is where they head. If the Spurs balance sheet would look better after a move away from Tottenham, then that becomes decisive. The fans who love their club and a neighbourhood that depends upon it become collateral damage in the scramble for shareholder value.

Club officials say that Spurs is "not a regeneration agency", and they are right. Those who run the game say that fans can always switch allegiances if they don't like the way they are treated. In theory, both have a point. But this is not how real life works. Proper fans don't change clubs in the same way they switch supermarkets. There is something important missing from the picture: the widespread conviction that though football clubs must compete, they should also be about something greater than profit and loss. No real fan would desert the club they love. Club executives know this. So the people who really make a football club – the fans – are left powerless.

The beguiling promise of the economic revolution of the 1980s was that free markets would mean free people. With the government out of the way, we would be able to make our own choices. No one would tell us where to shop, what to buy or who to work for. Armed with freedom, we would enter only into transactions that benefitted us. But when all you have is bad options, you are not powerful but powerless.

In theory, the River Heights families had a choice between defaulting on their mortgages or racking up interest – but that didn't feel like much of a choice to them. Spurs fans could have chosen another side if the club had moved across London against their wishes, but that would never feel the same as following the team they had grown up with. For others in Tottenham, the choice between a loan shark and paying the bills at the end of the month doesn't feel like a choice either. Nor does a choice between two bad jobs feel much like freedom.

These concerns go unrecognised in a politics premised on a version of economic freedom that has too little to say about the realities of power. People used to be told they had to accept whatever the state gave them: "The man in Whitehall knows best." Now we are told the same about market outcomes. For those like the River Heights families, politics has a new slogan: "The economist in Whitehall knows best."

Picking up the tab

Frequently it is the taxpayer who is left to pick up the tab when businesses become too mighty. Low pay now costs the taxpayer £6bn a year a year in benefits and forgone revenue.[8] Governments have scrambled to top up low pay through the benefits system while executive pay has soared. What has been neglected is the question of whether profits and power should be shared more widely within firms.

In the past, the government has tried to reward poorer families for making sacrifices in order to save,[9] but efforts to support thrift have been undermined by unscrupulous lenders dragging families back into debt. Some 200,000 households in Britain are now indebted to loan sharks, with surveys showing average interest rates of 825%.[10]

With energy prices soaring, governments have dispatched winter fuel payments to help pensioners heat their homes. These subsidies have helped but the real problem is that six big companies almost completely control the energy supply in Britain. This stranglehold prevents others from distributing energy at lower cost, allowing the big six to hike prices and announce record profits.

Public spending on housing benefit rose 50% in real terms in the last decade, costing the taxpayer more than the army and the navy combined.[11] But the increase wasn't simply to fund more homes: landlords have jacked up prices in the knowledge that councils have an obligation to house people. The result has been people on benefits being charged higher rents than those in work, often for worse accommodation – and an enormous bill for the taxpayer.[12]

In each case, the government has found itself doing more and more to repair the damage caused by the market. In each case, what has been missing has been a willingness to stand up to powerful interests.

Speed limits

Societies have always agreed ground rules for how their members make money. One person cannot sell a kidney to another even if that's what both parties want, for example. The purpose of a minimum wage is to prevent people from having to take jobs at exploitative rates. It is the responsibility of government to step in to prevent gross abuses of power in the marketplace.

Too often regulation is glibly dismissed as "red tape", when in fact it is an important way in which societies protect the weak from being bullied by the powerful. The River Heights families would have welcomed some red tape if it had helped them stand up to banks determined to squeeze every penny out of them. Many taxpayers might feel the same about the idea of new rules – such as rent controls – preventing unscrupulous landlords from milking the housing benefit system. The exploitation of the needy by loan sharks should have been stopped long ago by a cap on interest rates.[13]

Politics must rediscover the confidence to make decisions based explicitly on ethical grounds rather than defer to economic doctrines and frameworks to justify each and every decision. Proposals like rent controls or interest rate caps are the equivalent of speed limits on the roads. With a few more of them we might not require so many ambulances.

A voice

The morality of a society – and the marketplace within it – cannot be policed only from above, however. People need power in their own lives to stand up to unethical business practices as they see them.

In Tottenham, football fans have been fuming about the idea that Spurs might move to the Olympic stadium in Stratford.[14] They should have a proper voice in the running of their club. In Germany, 51% of the shares in top league clubs must be owned by supporters.[15] Barcelona, one of the world's leading clubs, is run by its 170,000 members, who elect the club president.[16] These are ideas we should be learning from in Britain. To help return the beautiful game to the people, 25% of shares should be reserved for democratically elected supporters' trusts.[17]

The lesson, especially for those who decry the number of rules and regulations handed down by government, is that when people have their own voice inside institutions then less red tape is required. In the workplace, for example, people should be given more opportunities to speak for themselves, rather than relying entirely on regulators to do the job for them. Unions perform this role in many workplaces, often brilliantly, but policy-makers could do more to encourage constructive dialogue between bosses and their employees. As is already the case in Germany, employees should be represented on the board of every large company.

More than three-quarters of the population believes the gap between high and low incomes is too large.[18] Six out of

10 agree that ordinary working people do not get their fair share of the nation's wealth.[19] These too are voices that should be heard in the nation's boardrooms. A new Freedom of Information Act for the private sector could require companies to publish pay ratios, showing the top, medium and bottom wages paid in the company. If boards really think the way they run their company is justifiable, then they should make their case to their customers and their shareholders.

An alternative

People are at their most powerful in markets, however, when they have many options to choose from. This is what stops companies from pushing their luck. For too long governments have been passive about demanding that there be real competition in sectors like banking and energy, where customers sense they are getting a raw deal but see little alternative.

What matters is not just the number of options, but their diversity. As any parent who has been "empowered" with the choice between two bad schools will recognise, real power comes only when there are genuinely different options to choose between. The River Heights families might not have been treated quite so ruthlessly, for example, by a bank owned and run in the interests of its customers.

However, following the wave of demutualisation in the 1980s, produced by Mrs Thatcher's free market reforms, our banks have become clones of one another, each adopting the shareholder model. In theory people have a choice between banks; in practice there is often very little difference. The reintroduction of building societies would help raise the bar again on how customers are treated by the organisations with which they bank. If a proper deal can be secured for taxpayers, for example, proposals for the remutualisation of Northern Rock should be taken up by the Treasury.

Likewise, the 200,000 British families indebted to loan sharks[20] might have thought twice about saying yes to doorstep lenders had they had another option. The typical low-income household could save £500 a year in debt repayments by borrowing money from a credit union,[21] an organisation owned by its members, in which savings from some members are used to offer loans to others along the cooperative model.[22] Capping interest rates is important to prevent exploitation, but giving people access to proper lines of credit is equally so. To support credit unions, local authorities and post offices around the country should be offering office space, training and help with back-office functions.

The surest way to reduce the power of slum landlords would be to build more houses. Even better than this, though, would be for those homes to be built on land owned in trust by the community itself. Under this model, the cost of land could be removed from the price of buying or renting homes, allowing prices to be held down permanently. To ensure more affordable housing, the government should not be selling off public land to developers, but rather placing it in trust to be owned by local communities.

The big economy

These ideas should be comfortable territory for a government that has promised to build a thriving society in which people take more power and responsibility over their own lives. What could be more "big society" than giving fans a role in running football clubs, employees a voice in the workplace, or customers a stake in their banks? Who could object to giving shareholders more information about the companies they own? Who would argue against government stepping in to promote more competition for customers in the marketplace? Though there will always be disagreements over the number of rules and regulations that an economy can sustain, giving ordinary people more power in the marketplace should be common ground.

It is not, however. For this government – and often for its predecessor – "empowerment" has been a word reserved for public service reform. What stands between the "big society" and the "big economy" is an impoverished notion of freedom, inherited from the economic revolution of the 1980s and insufficiently challenged by New Labour. It is that, above all, that must be challenged if people are to have any real power over their lives.

POSTSCRIPT

Never underestimate the cost of a riot. Just because the fires have been put out, the windows reglazed and the media satellite trucks have left does not mean the pain has ceased. Nor does the damage end when the last stone is thrown or the last shop looted. It continues when ordinary residents wake up to hear the name of their neighbourhood, often the place of their birth, dragged through the mud. Just 19 teenagers were arrested in Tottenham in conjunction with the riots, yet all 10,000 of Tottenham's teenagers will share the stigma and stereotyping that will inevitably follow.

Many businesses that were damaged or destroyed in the riots have yet to reopen. The wooden hoardings where people once made a living now haunt the High Road. Even businesses that had no damage done at all are on the brink of closure as shoppers steer clear of the neighbourhood.

Through no fault of their own, these brave, proud small business owners are staring bankruptcy and repossession in the face.

To have had two major riots within a generation is disastrous for one corner of London. It places Tottenham on a par with American hotspots like Detroit and South Central Los Angeles. A third riot would be catastrophic.

After the Broadwater Farm riots of 1985, Tottenham picked itself up. Away from the cameras, people worked hard at rebuilding their community. Policing became friendlier. Officers made themselves more approachable and relations slowly warmed.

But little else changed. Despite noble efforts to increase the number of jobs, unemployment remains stubbornly high. The justice system continues to churn out ex-prisoners who have been neither punished nor reformed. The absence of positive male role models in the lives of many young men is more acute today than it was in the 1980s. On top of this, the reach of street gangs and the pressures of consumer culture are more overbearing than ever. Successive governments have tried but never managed to change the truths echoed in reports like Faith in the City and A Study of Town Life: unemployment is high, work is insecure and wages are too low; families suffer and crime prevails.

For all this, Tottenham remains friendly and vibrant. The vast majority of residents want the same thing as everyone else – decency. A decent home, a decent job, decent opportunities for their children. The rioters don't represent Tottenham. Parents like my mum, taking on two jobs to give their children the best possible start in life – they represent Tottenham. Hard-working people like Mr Mufwankolo, building a business from scratch, and pledging to rebuild it after the riots – they represent Tottenham.

Writing this book gave me the opportunity to reflect on what I would have changed about my upbringing if I could, whether it be having my father for longer or being able to spend more time with my mother. The list was long – we are all entitled to regrets, after all – but the one thing I would never change is where I grew up.

While some centres of population are slowly morphing into clones of each other, Tottenham will always look and feel different. Despite the injustice of the situation that many of them find themselves in, and despite the terror of the riots, most people in Tottenham knuckle down and do the best they can for themselves and their families. This is what some outsiders do not understand about Tottenham or Salford or many of the other places that saw riots in the summer of 2011. They think that the riots define those communities – but those of us who were born there and live there know differently. The smoke and the stones can't obscure for ever the locals' strength of character.

But resilience alone is not enough. Those who put in so much over the past 26 years deserve answers – not just about why a second riot took place but about what will be done to prevent a third. Whatever some politicians might say, these riots were about more than "criminality, pure and simple". They were signposts to the failure of successive governments to answer the challenges of a new era of economic and social liberalism. Posturing about "broken" Britain and the "feral underclass" makes great headlines but remedies very little. We cannot live in a society in which the banks are too big to fail but whole communities are allowed to sink without a trace. Now is the time to start changing things.

NOTES

Introduction

1 K Stoddard, "Anger smoulders in Tottenham: the Broadwater farm riots of 1985", The Guardian Online, 8 August 2011, available at http://www.guardian.co.uk/theguardian/from-the-archive-blog/2011/aug/08/anger-tottenham-broadwater-riots-1985
2 J Booth, "When Tottenham rioted 26 years ago", The Times, 7 August 2011
3 Mid-Year Population Estimates, Office of National Statistics, http://www.ons.gov.uk
4 "Tottenham police shooting: dead man was minicab passenger", BBC News Online, 5 August 2011, available at http://www.bbc.co.uk/news/uk-england-london-14423942
5 "Ten arrested this year over PC Blakelock murder", BBC News Online, 6 October 2010, available at http://www.bbc.co.uk/news/uk-england-london-11484434
6 "1991: Silcott not guilty of PC's murder", BBC Online, available at http://news.bbc.co.uk/onthisday/hi/dates/stories/november/ 25/newsid_2546000/2546177.stm
7 D Hill, 'Words about Boris', Guardian Online, 21 Feb 2011, available at http://www.guardian.co.uk/politics/davehillblog/2011/feb/21/progressive-london-conference-verdict-on-boris-johnson Hansard 29 June 2010: Column 185WH, http://www.publications.parliament.uk/pa/cm201011/cmhansrd/cm100629/halltext/100629h0003.htm#10062943000201
8 "1985: Policeman killed in riots", BBC Online, available at http://news.bbc.co.uk/onthisday/hi/dates/stories/october/6/newsid_4094000/4094928.stm
9 "Arrest in Enfield Amid Looting And Violence", Sky News Online, 9 August 2011, available at http://news.sky.com/home/uk-news/article/16045049
10 J Halliday, "London rioters are not 'protestors' admits BBC", The Guardian, 10 August 2011, available at http://

www.guardian.co.uk/media/2011/aug/10/london-rioters-not-protesters-bbc

11 David Cameron speech to the Centre for Social Justice, 2006, full text available at http://news.bbc.co.uk/1/hi/5166498.stm
12 S Hattenstone, 'David Lammy: "There is a history in Tottenham that involves deaths in police custody"', The Guardian, 14 August 2011, available at http://www.guardian.co.uk/politics/2011/aug/14/david-lammy-tottenham-mark-duggan
13 "Toxteth's long road to recovery", BBC Online, 5 July 2001, available at http://news.bbc.co.uk/1/hi/uk/1416198.stm
14 "The Scarman Report", BBC Online, 27 April 2004, available at http://news.bbc.co.uk/1/hi/programmes/bbc_parliament/3631579.stm
15 The Broadwater farm inquiry – report of the independent inquiry chaired by Lord Gifford (1986)
16 "Race: the Macpherson report", BBC Online, 7 May 2001, available at http://news.bbc.co.uk/news/vote2001/hi/english/main_issues/sections/facts/newsid_1190000/1190971.stm

1. The thin blue line

1 The Communications Market: UK, Ofcom (2011), available at http://stakeholders.ofcom.org.uk/binaries/research/cmr/cmr11/UK_CMR_2011_FINAL.pdf
2 "Statistical bulletin on the public disorder of 6th-9th August 2011", Ministry of Justice, 24 October 2011, available at http://www.justice.gov.uk/publications/statistics-and-data/criminal-justice/public-disorder-august-11.htm
3 "Fightback! London's looters stay home as 16,000 police flood the streets ready to use plastic bullets", Daily Mail, 10 August 2011, available at: http://www.dailymail.co.uk/news/article-2023874/UK-riots-2011-16k-police-ready-use-plastic-bullets-lid-Londons-looters.html
4 "UK Riots: Police numbers boosted to 16,000", BBC News Online, 9 August 2011, available at http://www.bbc.co.uk/news/uk-14464799
5 "Police cuts 'to axe 16,00 posts' – Cardiff Uni report", BBC News Online, 16 August 2011, available at http://www.bbc.co.uk/news/uk-wales-14539976

6 M Easton, "Crime: do we need more police?", BBC Online, 28 April 2010, available at http://news.bbc.co.uk/1/hi/uk_politics/election_2010/parties_and_issues/8645379.stm
7 Kershaw, Nicholas & Walker (eds), "Crime in England and Wales 2007/08: Findings from the British Crime Survey and police recorded crime", The Home Office Statistical Bulletin, June 2008.
8 "Statistical bulletin on the public disorder of 6th-9th August 2011", Ministry of Justice, 24 October 2011, available at http://www.justice.gov.uk/publications/statistics-and-data/criminal-justice/public-disorder-august-11.htm
9 S Hunt (ed), Family Trends: British families since the 1950s, Family and Parenting Institute (2009), available at http://www.familyandparenting.org/familyTrends#2
10 Do Grandparents matter?, Family Matters Institute (2009), available at http://www.familymatters.org.uk/doc/Do_Grandparents_Matter.pdf
11 Anti-Social Behaviour Across Europe. ADT (2006)
12 R Bennett, "Children spend half as much time in class as they do looking at screens", The Times, 21 June 2009
13 The Children's Act, 2004
14 "Smacking children", House of Commons briefing note (2009), available at www.parliament.uk/briefing-papers/SN04710.pdf
15 R Reeves, S Sodha, "Bringing up baby", New Statesman, 29 Jan 2009, available at http://www.newstatesman.com/ideas/2009/01/parents-children-parenting
16 Written Parliamentary Question, Commons Hansard, Column 936W, 18th March 2008. available at http://www.publications.parliament.uk/pa/cm200708/cmhansrd/cm080318/text/80318w0002.htm
17 Green Paper Evidence Report, Breaking the Cycle: Effective punishment, rehabilitation and sentencing of offenders, Ministry of Justice (2009). available at http://www.justice.gov.uk/consultations/docs/green-paper-evidence-a.pdf
18 Reducing Re-offending by Ex-prisoners, Social Exclusion Unit (2002)
19 Back on track, Department for Children Schools and Families, 2008

20 Back on track, Department for Children Schools and Families, 2008
21 A Gilligan, "Tottenham and Broadwater Farm: a tale of two riots", Daily Telegraph Online, 7 August 2011, available at http://www.telegraph.co.uk/news/uknews/crime/8687879/Tottenham-and-Broadwater-Farm-A-tale-of-two-riots.html
22 A Gilligan, "Tottenham and Broadwater Farm: a tale of two riots", Daily Telegraph Online, 7 August 2011, available at http://www.telegraph.co.uk/news/uknews/crime/8687879/Tottenham-and-Broadwater-Farm-A-tale-of-two-riots.html
23 A Buonfino, L Thomposon, Belonging in contemporary Britain, Commission on integration and cohesion (2007), available at http://www.youngfoundation.org/files/images/belonging_in_contempary_britain_20pdf.pdf
24 "Unemployment benefit claimants constituency by constituency: full data", The Guardian Data Blog, available at http://www.guardian.co.uk/news/datablog/2010/nov/17/unemployment-and-employment-statistics-economics
25 Ben-Galim, Gottfried, "Exploring the relationship between riots areas and deprivation – an IPPR analysis", Institute of Public Policy Research, 16 August 2011, available at http://www.ippr.org/articles/56/7857/exploring-the-relationship-between-riot-areas-and-deprivation—an-ippr-analysis

2. Shameless

1 "PM Statement on violence in England", 10 August 2011, available at http://www.number10.gov.uk/news/pm-statement-on-violence-in-england/
2 K Clårke, "Punish the feral rioters, but address our social deficit too", Guardian, 5 September 2011, available at http://www.guardian.co.uk/commentisfree/2011/sep/05/punishment-rioters-help
3 "Riots 'justice wake-up call'", Evening Standard, 7 September 2011, available at http://www.thisislondon.co.uk/standard/article-23984077-riots-justice-system-wake-up-call.do
4 "Restoring fairness to the welfare system", Iain Duncan Smith speech, Conservative Party annual conference, 3 October 2011,

available at http://www.conservatives.com/News/Speeches/2011/10/Duncan_Smith_Restoring_fairness_to_the_welfare_system.aspx

5 Iain Duncan Smith, "We cannot arrest our way out of these riots", The Times, 15 September 2011

6 "PM Statement on restoring order to cities", 9 August 2011, http://www.number10.gov.uk/news/pm-statement-on-restoring-order/

7 Speech to the Conservative Party Conference, 10 October 1986, Margaret Thatcher, available at http://www.margaretthatcher.org/document/106498

8 M Whittaker, Missing Out, The Resolution Foundation (2011), available at http://www.resolutionfoundation.org/publications/missing-out/

9 Sir Paul Judge, "How we lost grip of top pay", Sunday Times, 14 November 2010

10 "More than a fifth of Britons have no savings", Daily Telegraph, 1 April 2010, available at http://www.telegraph.co.uk/finance/personalfinance/savings/7545194/More-than-a-fifth-of-Britons-have-no-savings.html

11 V Alakeson, "Making a rented house a home: housing solutions for 'generation rent'", Resolution Foundation (2011), available at http://www.resolutionfoundation.org/media/media/downloads/Housing_Report_Final.pdf

12 R Alleyne, "London riots: parents of young rioters don't care, says judge", Daily Telegraph, 13 August 2011, available at http://www.telegraph.co.uk/news/uknews/crime/8699194/London-riots-parents-of-young-rioters-dont-care-says-judge.html

13 R Phillips, "CBI defiantly opposes social chapter", The Independent, 11 May 1997, available at http://www.independent.co.uk/ news/business/cbi-defiantly-opposed-to-the-social-chapter-1260782.html

14 "CBI criticises government pledge to keep raising the minimum wage", Personnel Today, 30 September 2009, available http://www.personneltoday.com/articles/2009/09/30/52361/cbi-criticises-government-pledge-to-keep-raising-national-minimum.html

15 "CBI ends maternity leave support", BBC News Online, 23 September 2005, available at http://news.bbc.co.uk/1/hi/business/4555188.stm
16 A Grice, "CBI warns against flexible working", The Independent, 24 July 2008, available at http://www.independent.co.uk/news/uk/politics/cbi-warns-against-flexible-working-875761.html
17 "Extended parental leave 'will cause headache for HR', warns CBI", Personnel Today, 31 March 2009, available at http://www.personneltoday.com/articles/2009/03/31/50101/extended-parental-leave-will-cause-headache-for-hr-warns-cbi.html
18 "Cameron 'moral capitalism' plea", BBC News Online, 30 January 2009, available at http://news.bbc.co.uk/1/hi/business/davos/7860761.stm
19 L Savage, Low Pay Britain, Resolution Foundation (2011), available at http://www.resolutionfoundation.org/media/media/downloads/Low_Pay_Britain.pdf
20 YouGov Survey Results, 15-16 August 2011, available at http://today.yougov.co.uk/ sites/today.yougov.co.uk/files/yg-archives-yougov-brattonriots-170811.pdf
21 "The plan for social security: full outline", available at http://century.guardian.co.uk/1940-1949/Story/0,,127564,00.html
22 See G Cooke and P Gregg for a longer explanation of the different phases of development in Britain's welfare settlement
23 J Hills, Thatcher, New Labour and the Welfare, London School of Economics (1998), available at http://eprints.lse.ac.uk/5553/1/Thatcherism_New_Labour_and_the_Welfare_State.pdf
24 J Hills, Thatcher, New Labour and the Welfare, London School of Economics (1998), available at http://eprints.lse.ac.uk/5553/1/Thatcherism_New_Labour_and_the_Welfare_State.pdf
25 J Hills, Thatcher, New Labour and the Welfare, London School of Economics (1998), available at http://eprints.lse.ac.uk/5553/1/Thatcherism_New_Labour_and_the_Welfare_State.pdf
26 A Grice, "Brown Pledges a 'progressive' tax system", The Independent, 5 December 2000, available at http://www.independent.co.uk/news/uk/politics/brown-pledges-a-progressive-tax-system-627050.html
27 Meeting housing need: Building Britain out of recession, Unite

(2011), available at http://www.unitetheunion.org/pdf/Unite%20Meeting%20Housing%20Need.pdf
28 J Hills, Ends and Means: The future roles of social housing in England, LSE (2007), available at http://eprints.lse.ac.uk/5568/1/Ends_and_Means_The_future_roles_of_social_housing_in_England_1.pdf
29 J Hills, Ends and Means: The future roles of social housing in England, LSE (2007), available at http://eprints.lse.ac.uk/5568/1/Ends_and_Means_The_future_roles_of_social_housing_in_England_1.pdf
30 D Hencke, 'Only half of all vacancies are being advertised at job centres', Guardian, 18 March 2009, available at http://www.guardian.co.uk/politics/2009/mar/18/vanancies-jobcentres
31 V Alakeson, "Making a rented house a home: housing solutions for 'generation rent'", Resolution Foundation (2011), available at http://www.resolutionfoundation.org/media/media/downloads/Housing_Report_Final.pdf
32 V Alakeson, "Making a rented house a home: housing solutions for 'generation rent'", Resolution Foundation (2011), available at http://www.resolutionfoundation.org/media/media/downloads/Housing_Report_Final.pdf
33 V Alakeson, "Making a rented house a home: housing solutions for 'generation rent'", Resolution Foundation (2011), available at http://www.resolutionfoundation.org/media/media/downloads/Housing_Report_Final.pdf
34 "All about Community Land Trusts", The Guardian, 21 March 2007, available at http://www.guardian.co.uk/society/2007/mar/21/4?INTCMP=SRCH
35 For more details of the scheme see http://www.manchesterhomefinder.org/info/faqs/community.aspx

3. Nine to five

1 ONS Official Labour Market Statistics – www.nomisweb.co.uk
2 "Riot-hit London boroughs among the worst unemployment blackspots", The Guardian, 17/0802011 -http://www.guardian.co.uk/society/2011/aug/17/riot-hit-london-boroughs-unemployment

3 ONS Official Labour Market Statistics – www.nomisweb.co.uk
4 "Exploring the relationship between riot areas and deprivation – an IPPR analysis", IPPR, 16/08/2011 – http://www.ippr.org/articles/56/7857/exploring-the-relationship-between-riot-areas-and-deprivation—an-ippr-analysis
5 ONS Official Labour Market Statistics – www.nomisweb.co.uk
6 ONS Official Labour Market Statistics – www.nomisweb.co.uk
7 "Working and workless households, 2011" Office of National Statistics -http://www.ons.gov.uk/ons/rel/lmac/working-and-workless-households/2011/index.html
8 "Working and workless households, 2011" Office of National Statistics -http://www.ons.gov.uk/ons/rel/lmac/working-and-workless-households/2011/index.html
9 ONS Official Labour Market Statistics – www.nomisweb.co.uk
10 D Hirsch, J Beckhelling, "Tackling the adequacy gap: earnings, incomes and work incentives under the universal credit", Resolution Foundation (2011), available at: http://www.resolutionfoundation. org/media/media/downloads/BN_Tackling_the_adequacy_trap.pdf
11 IPPR, Structural Economic change and the European Union (2008) – http://www.ippr.org/images/media/files/publication/2011/ 05/Structural%20econ%20change%20and%20the%20EU_1670.pdf
12 M Brewer et al, Universal Credit: A preliminary analysis, Institute for Fiscal Studies (2010), available at http://www.ifs.org.uk/bns/bn116.pdf
13 For more on this proposal see S White, "Revolutionary Liberalism? The Philosophy and Politics of the Post War Liberal Party"
14 P Legrain, "Tax the Land they walk on", Prospect Magazine, Issue 169, available at http://www.prospectmagazine.co.uk/2010/03/tax-the-ground-they-walk-on-2/
15 P Legrain, "Tax the Land they walk on", Prospect Magazine, Issue 169, available at http://www.prospectmagazine.co.uk/2010/03/tax-the-ground-they-walk-on-2/
16 T Whitehead, "London riots: the 2012 Olympics ambassador turned in by her mother", Daily Telegraph, 12/08/2011 – http://www.telegraph.co.uk/news/uknews/crime/8696197/

London-riots-the-2012-Olympics-ambassador-turned-in-by-her-mother.html
17 M Friedman, "The Social Responsibility of Business is to Increase its Profits", New York Times Magazine, 13 September 1970, available at http://www.colorado.edu/studentgroups/libertarians/issues/friedman-soc-resp-business.html
18 C Leadbeater, Living on Thin Air: The New Economy, Penguin Books (1999)
19 "Mental Capital and well-being: making the most of ourselves in the 21st century", Government Office for Science (2008), available at http://www.foresight.gov.uk/Mental%20Capital/SR-C9_MCW.pdf
20 J Rutherford, "Class and Politics" (2008), available here: http://www.lwbooks.co.uk/journals/soundings/class_and_culture/article1.html
21 N Isles, The Joy of Work, Work Foundation (2004), available at http://www.theworkfoundation.com/research/publications/publicationdetail.aspx?oItemId=145
22 "Hard work, hidden lives: the full report of the commission on vulnerable employment", TUC (2009), available at http://www.vulnerableworkers.org.uk/files/CoVE_full_report.pdf
23 Leitch Review of Skills, "Skills in the UK: The long term challenge", interim report (London: HM Treasury, 2005)
24 R Page, Co-Determination in Germany (2009) http://www.boeckler.de/pdf/p_arbp_033.pdf
25 Centre for Economic Performance, UK Productivity during the Blair Era (undated) – http://cep.lse.ac.uk/briefings/pa_uk_productivity.pdf
26 Profit sharing in OECD countries, OECD, available at http://www.oecd.org/dataoecd/3/37/2409883.pdf

4. Boys' night out

1 "England riots: Court appearance total rises above 1,500", BBC News Online, 1 September 2011, available at http://www.bbc.co.uk/news/uk-14746229
2 "How fair is Britain: the first triennial review", Equality and Human Rights Commission (2010), available at http://

www.equalityhumanrights.com/key-projects/how-fair-is-britain/full-report-and-evidence-downloads/#How_fair_is_Britain_Equality_Human_Rights_and_Good_Relations_in_2010_The_First_Triennial_Review

3 "How fair is Britain: the first triennial review", Equality and Human Rights Commission (2010), available at http://www.equalityhumanrights.com/key-projects/how-fair-is-britain/full-report-and-evidence-downloads/#How_fair_is_Britain_Equality_Human_Rights_and_Good_Relations_in_2010_The_First_Triennial_Review
4 "How fair is Britain: the first triennial review", Equality and Human Rights Commission (2010), available at http://www.equalityhumanrights.com/key-projects/how-fair-is-britain/full-report-and-evidence-downloads/#How_fair_is_Britain_Equality_Human_Rights_and_Good_Relations_in_2010_The_First_Triennial_Review
5 Unpublished figures from the Haringey Young Offenders Service
6 S Hunt (ed), Family Trends: British families since the 1950s, Family and Parenting Institute (2009), available at http://www.familyandparenting.org/familyTrends#2
7 "Parents face fees for child maintenance rulings", BBC News Online, 13 January 2011, available at http://www.bbc.co.uk/news/uk-politics-12174121
8 "Women and Children's poverty: making the links", Oxfam (2005), available at http://www.oxfam.org.uk/resources/ukpoverty/downloads/WBGWomensandchildrenspoverty.pdf
9 Research Summary: separated families, Fatherhood Institute, available at http://www.fatherhoodinstitute.org/2008/fi-research-summary-separated-families/
10 Rob William essay, "Where Next for Parenting", Family and Parenting Institute (2011)
11 Research Summary: separated families, Fatherhood Institute, available at http://www.fatherhoodinstitute.org/2008/fi-research-summary-separated-families/
12 S Hunt (ed), Family Trends: British families since the 1950s, Family and Parenting Institute (2009), available at http://www.familyandparenting.org/familyTrends#2

13 S Hunt (ed), Family Trends: British families since the 1950s, Family and Parenting Institute (2009), available at http://www.familyandparenting.org/familyTrends#2
14 Working Better: Fathers families work, Research Report, Equality and Human Rights Commission (2008), available at http://www.equalityhumanrights.com/uploaded_files/research/41_wb_fathers_family_and_work.pdf
15 "One in four primary schools still has no male teachers", BBC News Online, 2 September 2011, http://www.bbc.co.uk/news/education-14748273
16 Giggs, Hollowman – http://www.youtube.com/watch?v=AUW3_cTeDbk
17 "Police identify 169 London gangs", BBC News, 21 February 2007, available at http://news.bbc.co.uk/1/hi/england/london/6383933.stm
18 Shot in the shoulder, he went on to make a full recovery

5. Loot

1 "JD Sports says rioters looted £700,000 of stock", BBC News Online, 21/09/2011 – http://www.bbc.co.uk/news/business-14998770
2 Layard, Happiness, Wilson and Picket, The Sprit Level
3 Positional Goods: New inequalities and the importance of relative position, Young Foundation (2006), available at http://www.youngfoundation.org/files/images/The_value_of_positional_goods.pdf
4 "UK work week among EU's longest", BBC News Online, 4 September 2008, available at http://news.bbc.co.uk/1/hi/7598467.stm
5 E Conway, "British household debt highest in history", 28 June 2008, Daily Telegraph, available at http://www.telegraph.co.uk/finance/2792372/British-household-debt-is-highest-in-history.html
6 Dr T Morgan, Thinking the unthinkable, Tullet Prebon (2011), available at http://www.tullettprebon.com/Documents/strategyinsights/Tim_Morgan_Report_007.pdf

7 R Dobson, "Stress due to mounting debt costs the NHS millions", Daily Telegraph, 25 October 2008, available at http://www.telegraph.co.uk/health/3257875/Stress-due-to-mounting-debt-costs-NHS-millions.html
8 D Lammy, Steven Lawrence Lecture, 16 September 2004
9 E Mayo, A Nairn, Consumer Kids: How Big Business Is Grooming Our Children for Profit, Constable (2009)
10 Agnes Naim, Business thinks family, Parenting and family institute (2008), available at http://www.familyandparenting.org/Filestore/Documents/publications/Business_Thinks_Family_FINAL.pdf
11 Polling available at http://www.commonsensemedia.org/about-us/press-room/press-releases/online-privacy-poll
12 "Promote your business with ads", Facebook, available at http://www.facebook.com/business/ads/
13 "Facebook snubs panic button call by Home Secretary", Daily Mail, 19 March 2010, available at http://www.dailymail.co.uk/news/article-1258914/Facebook-objection-installing-panic-button-meeting-Home-Secretary-Alan-Johnson.html
14 "The targeting I want isn't available", Facebook, available at http://www.facebook.com/help/?faq=146980428707632
15 "The commercialisation of childhood", Compass (2007), available at http://clients.squareeye.com/uploads/compass/documents/thecommercialisationofchildhood.pdf
16 Prof C Pole, New Consumers? Children, fashion and consumption; School of Social Science, Nottingham Trent University.
17 "The commercialisation of childhood", Compass (2007), available at http://clients.squareeye.com/uploads/compass/documents/thecommercialisationofchildhood.pdf
18 Digital Data Bill – http://kerry.senate.gov/imo/media/doc/Commercial%20Privacy%20Bill%20of%20Rights%20Text.pdf
19 "Sweden pushes for ad ban", BBC News Online, 13/02/2001 – http://news.bbc.co.uk/1/hi/world/europe/1167723.stm
20 "Visual Pollution", The Economist. 11 October 2007, available at http://www.economist.com/node/9963268
21 "Can you manufacture good character?", BBC News Online Magazine, 09/07/2008 – http://news.bbc.co.uk/1/hi/magazine/7497081.stm

22 "England riots: debate over clean-up costs", BBC News Online, 20 August 2011, available at http://www.bbc.co.uk/news/business-14590252

6. Rights and wrongs

1 Dr J Oldfield, "British Anti-Slavery", BBC Online, available at http://www.bbc.co.uk/history/british/empire_seapower/antislavery_01.shtml
2 "Focus on the slave trade", BBC Online, available at http://news.bbc.co.uk/1/hi/world/africa/1523100.stm
3 C Brown, "Blair admits to 'deep sorrow' over slavery – but no apology", The Independent, 26 November 2006 http:/www.independent.co.uk/news/uk/politics/blair-admits-to-deep-sorrow-over-slavery—but-no-apology-426058.html
4 "Women: From Abolition to the Vote", BBC Online, available at http://www.bbc.co.uk/history/british/abolition/abolition_women_article_01.shtml
5 N Temko, J Doward, "Revealed: Blair attack on human rights law", The Guardian, 14 May 2006, available at http://www.guardian.co.uk/politics/2006/may/14/humanrights.ukcrime
6 K Kaur Ballagan et al, Public perceptions of human rights, MORI/EHRC (2009), available at http://www.equalityhumanrights.com/uploaded_files/public_perceptions_of_human_rights_ipos_mori.pdf
7 Ben Page interview, "Social attitudes towards political equality", December 2008, available at http://www.idea.gov.uk/idk/core/page.do?pageId=9193774
8 YouGov/ITV survey results, 2011, available at http://today.yougov.co.uk/sites/today.yougov.co.uk/files/yg-archives-pol-yougovitv-humanrights-240311.pdf
9 "PM Statement on violence in England", 10 August 2011, available at http://www.number10.gov.uk/news/pm-statement-on-violence-in-england/
10 "PM's speech on the fightback after the riots", 15 August 2011, available at http://www.number10.gov.uk/news/pms-speech-on-the-fightback-after-the-riots/

11 "PM's statement on Libya", 22 August 2011, available at http://www.number10.gov.uk/news/pms-statement-on-libya/
12 C Gearty, "Human rights are only universal if we make them so", available at http://therightsfuture.com/t3-making-truth/
13 A Hirsch, "Bad press: human rights myths exposed", The Guardian Online, available at http://www.guardian.co.uk/humanrightsandwrongs/bad-press
14 "Review of the implementation of the human rights act", Department for Constitutional Affairs (2006), available at http://www.justice.gov.uk/guidance/docs/full_review.pdf
15 Integrated strategy against violence, Council of Europe (2009), available at http://www.coe.int/t/transversalprojects/children/News/Guidelines/Recommendation%20CM%20A4%20protection%20of%20children%20_ENG_BD.pdf
16 L Elliot, P Wintour, "Darling announces one-off tax to 'break bonus culture'", The Guardian, 7 December 2009, available in http://www.guardian.co.uk/uk/2009/dec/07/alistair-darling-shock-tax-bankers
17 House of Commons, 3 November 2010, Hansard, http://www.publications.parliament.uk/pa/cm201011/cmhansrd/cm101103/debtext/101103-0001.htm
18 "MPs reject prisoner votes plan", BBC News Online, 10 February 2011, available at http://www.bbc.co.uk/news/uk-politics-12409426
19 A Horne, The changing constitution: a case for judicial confirmation hearings?, Home Affairs Research Section, House of Commons (2010), available at http://www.spg.org.uk/spg-paper-1.pdf
20 E Skidelsky, "The return of goodness", Prospect Magazine, Issue 150, 28 September 2008, available at http://www.prospectmagazine.co.uk/2008/09/thereturnofgoodness/
21 M A Glendon, Rights Talk: the impoverishment of political discourse (1994)

7. Banged up

1 G Berman, Prison population statistics, parliamentary briefing paper (2011), available at www.parliament.uk/briefing-papers/SN04334.pdf

2 G Berman, Prison population statistics, parliamentary briefing paper (2011), available at www.parliament.uk/briefing-papers/SN04334.pdf
3 Prison Reform Working Group, "Locked up potential", Centre for Social Justice, (2009) – http://www.centreforsocialjustice.org.uk/client/downloads/CSJLockedUpPotentialFULLrEPORT.pdf
4 G Berman, Prison population statistics, parliamentary briefing paper (2011), available at www.parliament.uk/briefing-papers/SN04334.pdf
5 K Clarke, "Punish the feral rioters, but address our social deficit too", The Guardian, 05/09/2011 – http://www.guardian.co.uk/commentisfree/2011/sep/05/punishment-rioters-help
6 "Statistical bulletin on the public disorder of 6th to 9th August 2011", Ministry of Justice Statistics bulletin, 15/09/2011 – http://www.justice.gov.uk/downloads/publications/statistics-and-data/mojstats/august-public-disorder-stats-bulletin.pdf
7 "Statistical bulletin on the public disorder of 6th to 9th August 2011", Ministry of Justice Statistics bulletin, 15/09/2011 – http://www.justice.gov.uk/downloads/publications/statistics-and-data/mojstats/august-public-disorder-stats-bulletin.pdf
8 "Justice Secretary plans 'radical' prison policy change", BBC News Online, 30/06/2011 – http://www.bbc.co.uk/news/10457112
9 Ken Clarke Speech, Centre for crime and justice studies, 30 June 2010
10 D Cascani, Analysis: Cutting prison numbers, BBC News Online, available at, http://www.bbc.co.uk/news/uk-11929537
11 "Justice Secretary plans 'radical' prison policy change", BBC News Online, 30/06/2011 – http://www.bbc.co.uk/news/10457112
12 "Man jailed for Facebook incitement to riot to appeal", BBC News Online, 17/08/2011 – http://www.bbc.co.uk/news/uk-england-14557772
13 J Cooper, "Riots have led to a disproportionate increase in sentencing", The Guardian, 09/09/2011 – http://www.guardian.co.uk/commentisfree/libertycentral/2011/sep/09/riots-disproportionate-increase-sentencing
14 Lord Ashcroft, Crime, Punishment & The People (2011), available at http://www.lordashcroft.com/pdf/03042011_crime_punishment_and_the_people.pdf

15 Lord Ashcroft, Crime, Punishment & The People (2011), available at http://www.lordashcroft.com/pdf/03042011_crime_punishment_and_the_people.pdf
16 Lord Ashcroft, Crime, Punishment & The People (2011), available at http://www.lordashcroft.com/pdf/03042011_crime_punishment_and_the_people.pdf
17 D Damon, "Lessons from Danish prisons", BBC News Online, 2 July 2003, available at http://news.bbc.co.uk/1/hi/world/europe/3036450.stm
18 Prison Policy Update Briefing Paper, Ministry of Justice, April 2008. http://www.justice.gov.uk/publications/docs/prison-policy-update.pdf
19 Ministry of Justice, Research Summary 5, Factors linked to re-offending, Home Office (2008)
20 K Barney, "New wing aims to break cycle of teenage crime", Evening Standard, 5 November 2009 – http://www.thisislondon.co.uk/standard/article-23764797-new-wing-aims-to-break-cycle-of-teenage-crime.do
21 D Cascani, Analysis: Cutting prison numbers, BBC News Online, available at, http://www.bbc.co.uk/news/uk-11929537
22 D Cascani, Analysis: Cutting prison numbers, BBC News Online, available at, http://www.bbc.co.uk/news/uk-11929537
23 "Short-term prisoner reoffending "costs economy £10 billion", BBC News Online, 10 March 2010, available at http://news.bbc.co.uk/1/hi/uk/8558802.stm
24 A Travis, "Will social impact bonds solve society's most intractable problems?", The Guardian, 6 October 2010, available at http://www.guardian.co.uk/society/2010/oct/06/social-impact-bonds-intractable-societal-problems

8. Black and white

1 "The BNP: Anti-asylum protest, racist sect or power-winning movement?", BNP website, available at http://web.archive.org/web/20071010043702/http://www.bnp.org.uk/articles/race_reality.htm
2 Results for Leicestershire North West available at BBC News Online – http://news.bbc.co.uk/1/shared/election2010/results/ constituency/d32.stm

3 N Lowles, "We did it", Hope Not Hate blog, 08/05/2010 – http://www.hopenothate.org.uk/blog/article/753/we-did-it
4 N Lowles, "We did it", Hope Not Hate blog, 08/05/2010 – http://www.hopenothate.org.uk/blog/article/753/we-did-it
5 "Vote 2011: BNP suffers council seat losses", BBC News Online, 6 May 2011 – http://www.bbc.co.uk/news/uk-politics-13313069
6 J Darlington, "Enfield Town community forms 'vigilante' group", Enfield Independent, 10 August 2011 – http://www.enfieldindependent.co.uk/news/9186023.Enfield_Town_community_forms__vigilante__group/
7 J Darlington, "Enfield Town community forms 'vigilante' group", Enfield Independent, 10 August 2011 – http://www.enfieldindependent.co.uk/news/9186023.Enfield_Town_community_forms__vigilante__group/
8 Williams, Kisiel, Camber, "Right-wing extremists hijacking the vigilante patrols protecting against looters, warn police", Daily Mail, 11 August 2011 – http://www.dailymail.co.uk/news/article-2024707/UK-riots-2011-Met-Polices-Tim-Godwin-warns-EDL-hijack-vigilante-patrols.html?ito=feeds-newsxml
9 Beaumont, Coleman, Laville, "London riots: 'people are fighting back. It's their neighbourhoods at stake", The Guardian, – http://www.guardian.co.uk/uk/2011/aug/09/london-riots-fighting-neighbourhoods
10 Taken from BNP leaflet, available here: http://www.bnp.org.uk/sites/default/files/britainstripped_a4_mono_3.pdf
11 "Statistical bulletin on the public disorder of 6th-9th August 2011", Ministry of Justice, 24 October 2011, available at http://www.justice.gov.uk/publications/statistics-and-data/criminal-justice/public-disorder-august-11.htm
12 Taken from BNP leaflet, available here: http://www.bnp.org.uk/sites/default/files/britainstripped_a4_mono_3.pdf
13 "Reclaiming the streets: Sikhs defend their temples and locals protect their pubs as ordinary Britons defy the rioters", Daily Mail, 10/08/2011 – http://www.dailymail.co.uk/news/article-2024358/UK-RIOTS-2011-Sikhs-defend-temple-locals-protect-pubs-Britons-defy-rioters.html

14 R Syal, "Father of man killed in Birmingham riots speaks of faith in local community", The Guardian, 12/08/2011 – http://www.guardian.co.uk/uk/2011/aug/12/birmingham-riots-tariq-jahan
15 "Police pledge over Lozells peace five years after riots", BBC News Online, 22/10/2010 – uk-england-birmingham-11610159
16 "Funeral held for riot car victims", Press Association, http://www.pressassociation.com/component/pafeeds/2011/08/18/funerals_held_for_riot_car_victims?camefrom=home
17 S Lee, Do the right thing (1989) – http://www.imdb.com/title/tt0097216/
18 P Haggis, Crash (2004) – http://www.imdb.com/title/tt0375679/fullcredits
19 S Alinsky, Rules for radicals: A pragmatic primer for realistic radicals, Random House (1989)
20 MORI monthly polls, quoted in D Halpern, The Hidden Wealth of Nations, Polity (2009)
21 MORI monthly polls, quoted in D Halpern, The Hidden Wealth of Nations, Polity (2009)
22 "Immigration points system begins, BBC News Online, 29 February 2008, available at http://news.bbc.co.uk/1/hi/7269790.stm
23 "UK jobs open to migrants unveiled", BBC News Online, 11 November 2008, available at http://news.bbc.co.uk/1/hi/7722196.stm
24 J Rutter, M Latorre, Social housing allocation and immigrant communities, IPPR (2009)
25 Irregular Migration in the UK: an IPPR factfile, IPPR (2006) http://www.ippr.org/publicationsandreports/publication.asp?id=446
26 2001 Census, data available at www.nomisweb.co.uk
27 Citizenship Survey: April-September 2010, England, Department for Communities and Local government, available at http://www.communities.gov.uk/documents/statistics/pdf/1815799.pdf

9. Banks and bureaucrats

1 Haringey council website, available at http://www.haringey.gov.uk/housingoptions

2 D Jestico, "Repairs to 11,000 Haringey homes put on hold for another year", Tottenham & Wood Green Journal, 07/07/2011 – http://www.tottenhamjournal.co.uk/news/repairs_to_11_000_haringey_homes_put_on_hold_for_another_year_1_956459
3 "New police commissioners 'could cost more than £136m'," BBC News Online, 1 December 2010, available at http://www.bbc.co.uk/news/uk-11882026
4 All reports are available on the IPPC website – http://www.ipcc.gov.uk/en/Pages/reports_polcustody.aspx
5 "Taxpayers bailout 'justified' says NAO", BBC News Online, 4 December 2009, available at http://news.bbc.co.uk/1/hi/8394393.stm
6 M Glasman "Labour as a radical tradition", Soundings (2011), available at http://www.lwbooks.co.uk/journals/soundings/articles/s46glasman.pdf
7 Tottenham Hotspur history – http://tottenhamhotspur2.com/history.html
8 M Brewer, D Phillips, IFS Analysis on the Living Wage, Institute of Fiscal Studies, (2010), available at http://www.ifs.org.uk/publications/5244
9 The "Savings Gateway" would have seen the government add 50p to every £1 saved by families earning less that £15,000 a year but it was scrapped in June 2010 before a single penny was spent.
10 L Bachelor, "Loan sharks target poorest households with 825% APR loans", The Guardian, 15 January 2010, available at http://www.guardian.co.uk/money/2010/jan/15/loan-sharks-poorest-households
11 P Aldrick, "Lord Freud: Housing benefit landlords are ripping off the system", The Telegraph, 17 October 2011 http://www.telegraph.co.uk/finance/economics/8069810/Lord-Freud-Housing-benefit-landlords-are-ripping-off-the-system.html
12 P Aldrick, "Lord Freud: Housing benefit landlords are ripping off the system", The Telegraph, 17 October 2011 http://www.telegraph.co.uk/finance/economics/8069810/Lord-Freud-Housing-benefit-landlords-are-ripping-off-the-system.html
13 Stella Creasey MP has led the field on this issue.
14 At the time of writing, the outcome of this proposal was unclear.

15 D Conn, "Bundesliga votes to keep clubs owned by members", The Guardian, 13 November 2009 – http://www.guardian.co.uk/sport/david-conn-inside-sport-blog/2009/nov/13/bundesligafootball-bayernmunich

16 P French, "Clubs owned and run by their members are already a European reality", The Guardian, 20 December 2005, available at http://www.guardian.co.uk/football/2005/dec/20/europeanfootball.sport

17 D Mentipy, "Putting mutualism back at the heart of football", LabourList – http://www.labourlist.org/putting-mutualism-back-at-the-heart-of-football

18 British Social Attitudes survey – http://www.britsocat.com/Body.aspx?control=HomePage,

19 British Social Attitudes survey – http://www.britsocat.com/Body.aspx?control=HomePage,

20 L Bachelor, "Loan sharks target poorest households with 825% APR loans", The Guardian, 15 January 2010, available at http://www.guardian.co.uk/money/2010/jan/15/loan-sharks-poorest-households

21 L Bachelor, "Loan sharks target poorest households with 825% APR loans", The Guardian, 15 January 2010, available at http://www.guardian.co.uk/money/2010/jan/15/loan-sharks-poorest-households

22 L Bachelor, "Loan sharks target poorest households with 825% APR loans", The Guardian, 15 January 2010, available at http://www.guardian.co.uk/money/2010/jan/15/loan-sharks-poorest-households

ACKNOWLEDGEMENTS

My biggest thanks go to the people of Tottenham, whose stories and experiences are the reason for this book. All of my proceeds from it will go to charities working on post-riot issues in the constituency.

Much of the text and shape of this book would not exist without the hard work and fine mind of Duncan O'Leary. Thank you for believing in me, even if sometimes I doubted myself, and most of all for giving up so much of your life, your evenings, weekends and holidays to research, draft and revise this material.

It would have been impossible to write this without the discreet and dedicated team who have made up my office over the years. Thank you, Pier Barrett, for your tenacious research and investigative skills. Thank you Phil Glanville, Sam Hinton-Smith, Maxine Lyseight, Jen McClafferty, Nora Mulready, Senay Nihat, Emma Plunkett, Lindsey Rostron, Mark Rusling, Tom Stoate, Tom Tábori, Emma Taggart and Robin Todd. Thank you for everything – but above all for serving the people of Tottenham.

Alan Rusbridger had faith in this project long before the issues felt current or mainstream. Thank you for sticking with me.

David Matthews, thank you for helping me with the genesis of this project. Sarah Pyper, thank you for sharing your eye for language and wealth of experience. Eileen Horne, I am so grateful for your red pen and your ideas and for opening up your contact book.

Kate Critchley, Lara Pawson, Miranda Pyne, Vicky Coren, David Cummings, Sabrina Broadbent and Georgia Garrett all read early drafts and sections of manuscripts. I am profoundly grateful for your suggestions.

Ideas are hard to come by, and many minds have inspired me in this book. Thank you Tom Bentley, David Coats, Graeme Cooke, Jon Cruddas, Will Davies, Maurice Glasman, David Goodhart, Tristram Hunt, Will Hutton, Sunder Katwala, David Miliband, Geoff Mulgan, Robin Murray, Penny Nicholson, Nick Pearce, Carlota Perez, Jonathan Rutherford, Marc Stears, Matthew Taylor, Chuka Umunna, Stuart White and Stewart Wood.

Many thanks to Waheed Alli, Sue and Clive Hollick and Alison Parente, who have been so generous with their support.

My thanks to Katie Roden and Sara Montgomery at Guardian Books, to Nigel Wilcockson and Najma Finlay at Random House, to Phil Daoust, who has edited this book to tight deadlines so diligently, and to my agent Andrew Gordon.

To my old friends who knew me long before I came into politics, thank you for calling me Dave. If I have remained sane in the more stressful moments, it is because of you.

I am blessed with a family that propels me to be all I can be. To my darling wife Nicola, thank you for your wells of love and your assistance in putting my armour on each morning and taking it off at the end of each day. Joshua and Theo, you now have Daddy back a bit! To my siblings Carl, Lavine, Des and Ian, thank you for your patience and understanding. To Malcom and Julie, thank you for your surrogate love and endless optimism.

Thank you.

INDEX

(the initials DL in subentries refer to David Lammy)